UNDERSTANDING JONATHAN LETHEM

UNDERSTANDING CONTEMPORARY AMERICAN LITERATURE

Matthew J. Bruccoli, Founding Editor

Linda Wagner-Martin, Series Editor

Volumes on

Edward Albee | Sherman Alexie | Nelson Algren | Paul Auster
Nicholson Baker | John Barth | Donald Barthelme | The Beats
Thomas Berger | The Black Mountain Poets | Robert Bly | T. C. Boyle
Truman Capote | Raymond Carver | Michael Chabon | Fred Chappell
Chicano Literature | Contemporary American Drama
Contemporary American Horror Fiction
Contemporary American Literary Theory
Contemporary American Science Fiction, 1926–1970
Contemporary American Science Fiction, 1970–2000
Contemporary Chicana Literature | Pat Conroy | Robert Coover | Don DeLillo
Philip K. Dick | James Dickey | E. L. Doctorow | Rita Dove | Dave Eggers
John Gardner | George Garrett | Tim Gautreaux | John Hawkes | Joseph Heller Lillian
Hellman | Beth Henley | James Leo Herlihy | David Henry Hwang
John Irving | Randall Jarrell | Charles Johnson | Diane Johnson
Adrienne Kennedy | William Kennedy | Jack Kerouac | Jamaica Kincaid
Etheridge Knight | Tony Kushner | Ursula K. Le Guin | Jonathan Lethem
Denise Levertov | Bernard Malamud | David Mamet | Bobbie Ann Mason
Colum McCann | Cormac McCarthy | Jill McCorkle | Carson McCullers
W. S. Merwin | Arthur Miller | Stephen Millhauser | Lorrie Moore
Toni Morrison's Fiction | Vladimir Nabokov | Gloria Naylor | Joyce Carol Oates
Tim O'Brien | Flannery O'Connor | Cynthia Ozick | Suzan-Lori Parks | Walker Percy
Katherine Anne Porter | Richard Powers | Reynolds Price | Annie Proulx
Thomas Pynchon | Theodore Roethke | Philip Roth | Richard Russo | May Sarton
Hubert Selby, Jr. | Mary Lee Settle | Sam Shepard | Neil Simon
Isaac Bashevis Singer | Jane Smiley | Gary Snyder | William Stafford
Robert Stone | Anne Tyler | Gerald Vizenor | Kurt Vonnegut
David Foster Wallace | Robert Penn Warren | James Welch | Eudora Welty
Edmund White | Colson Whitehead | Tennessee Williams
August Wilson | Charles Wright

UNDERSTANDING JONATHAN LETHEM

Matthew Luter

The University of South Carolina Press

Published by the University of South Carolina Press
Columbia, South Carolina 29208

www.sc.edu/uscpress

Manufactured in the United States of America

24 23 22 21 20 19 18 17 16 15
10 9 8 7 6 5 4 3 2 1

Library of Congress Cataloging-in-Publication Data
can be found at http://catalog.loc.gov/.

ISBN 978-1-61117-512-7 (cloth)
ISBN 978-1-61117-513-4 (ebook)

This book was printed on recycled paper with
30 percent postconsumer waste content.

For everyone who has ever recommended a book, movie, or record to me
and for those loved ones of mine for whom I have done the same

CONTENTS

SERIES EDITOR'S PREFACE

The Understanding Contemporary American Literature series was founded by the estimable Matthew J. Bruccoli (1931–2008), who envisioned these volumes as guides or companions for students as well as good nonacademic readers, a legacy that will continue as new volumes are developed to fill in gaps among the nearly one hundred series volumes published to date and to embrace a host of new writers only now making their marks on our literature.

As Professor Bruccoli explained in his preface to the volumes he edited, because much influential contemporary literature makes special demands, "the word understanding in the titles was chosen deliberately. Many willing readers lack an adequate understanding of how contemporary literature works; that is, of what the author is attempting to express and the means by which it is conveyed." Aimed at fostering this understanding of good literature and good writers, the criticism and analysis in the series provide instruction in how to read certain contemporary writers—explicating their material, language, structures, themes, and perspectives—and facilitate a more profitable experience of the works under discussion.

In the twenty-first century Professor Bruccoli's prescience gives us an avenue to publish expert critiques of significant contemporary American writing. The series continues to map the literary landscape and to provide both instruction and enjoyment. Future volumes will seek to introduce new voices alongside canonized favorites, to chronicle the changing literature of our times, and to remain, as Professor Bruccoli conceived, contemporary in the best sense of the word.

Linda Wagner-Martin, Series Editor

ACKNOWLEDGMENTS

I must first express my appreciation to Linda Wagner-Martin, for support, encouragement, and irreplaceable editorial insight throughout the process of creating this book, and to Jim Denton and Linda Haines Fogle at the University of South Carolina Press for the opportunity to have my work appear in such an esteemed series.

Many thanks to my family and their continued interest in what I am reading and thinking. Though they may not remember it as well as I do, when I was in college and graduate school with no great amount of pocket money, they often bought me new books by Lethem in hardcover to spare me the impatient wait for the paperbacks. Please consider this book a return on your investment from several years ago.

Thanks as well to the many close friends who have checked in on me, cheered me on, and, sometimes, cheered me up as I have researched and written this book, including several who have become fellow Lethem readers. Cliché as it is to say, I could not have done it without you.

My appreciation to my colleagues and the administrators at the Webb School of Knoxville for helping make it possible to complete a book while facing the challenges of starting a new job on a new campus in a new city.

I have also had the good fortune to teach Lethem's work, particularly *The Fortress of Solitude* and "The Ecstasy of Influence," to bright and talented students at UNC–Chapel Hill and Davidson College. Their reactions, insights, and good-humored class discussion have been invaluable to me as I've formed, shared, and tested my own interpretations of Lethem's work—my thanks to them.

Thanks go to all of the critics, readers, and reviewers thinking aloud about Lethem in print, and especially James Peacock, for starting a wonderful critical on-the-page conversation that I feel honored to continue here.

And to Lethem himself, for Conrad Metcalf, Sergius Gogan, and everything in between.

ABBREVIATIONS

Textual references to Lethem's work and to his statements in interviews are cited parenthetically in text using the abbreviations below.

CC	*Chronic City*
Conv	*Conversations with Jonathan Lethem*
DG	*Dissident Gardens*
FoM	*Fear of Music*
MB	*Motherless Brooklyn*
TDA	*The Disappointment Artist*
TEoI	*The Ecstasy of Influence*
TFoS	*The Fortress of Solitude*

CHAPTER 1

Understanding Jonathan Lethem

Jonathan Lethem's popularity with critics, reviewers, and readers has steadily increased over the two-decade period he has been publishing fiction and essays. His versatility as a critic and wide range of artistic interests make his worldview particularly appealing to culturally omnivorous readers, those who see no cognitive dissonance in reading high modernism by day and watching horror flicks by night. Examples of his culturally omnivorous output would include music writing for *Rolling Stone,* a 2007–8 ten-issue revival of the 1970s comic book *Omega the Unknown,* a pseudonymous sports-novel-parody about the New York Mets, and a book-length sort-of-academic study of a 1980s satirical action flick that starred a pro wrestler. As a result of this eclecticism, Lethem's body of work can seem unwieldy and even intimidating to new readers, however, so a goal in this book is to arrange Lethem's major fiction and essays so that a few key recurring concerns can be highlighted and traced over the course of a career.

The body of criticism about Lethem's work is currently small but rapidly growing. For all the attention that Lethem's work receives in the literary press and for all his status as a major contemporary American novelist, there is as of yet only one previous book-length study of Lethem's work. James Peacock's monograph *Jonathan Lethem* (2012) uses genre as a lens for interpretation of every Lethem novel up to and including *Chronic City.* Given that Lethem began his career and found his initial literary successes as a writer of science fiction, Peacock's focus on genre is apt. By all means, that critical lens is useful, given how adeptly and frequently Lethem has borrowed the conventions of various forms of genre fiction: the western, sci-fi, the detective novel, dystopian fiction, and the coming-of-age novel, just to name a few. He knows these popular forms well, and he defends and reinvigorates them in his own work, all the while refusing to consider these popular modes of fiction less significant than the grand tradition outside of which they usually operate. He writes for posterity and takes literary history and criticism seriously, but he has also written and spoken frequently about the formative experience of voraciously reading—and unapologetically loving—genre fiction, particularly sci-fi and detective novels.

Borrowing openly and promiscuously from earlier traditions both high and low, Lethem displays a career-long interest in questioning what literary originality means in a postmodern age. After all, the dominant mode of creation of the late twentieth and early twenty-first centuries now appears to be appropriation and reuse of the creativity of one's forebears: depending on the decade, call it collage, pop art, pastiche, remixing, or sampling. Given this possibility that we may all now add up to little more than the sum of our influences, many have suggested that originality is overrated, undesirable, or maybe even impossible. As a result Lethem's career intervenes in one of the definitive academic debates in the field of contemporary and postmodern fiction: is this writer giving us anything genuinely original, or is this mere pastiche, just a reworking of existing material dressed up in newly hip clothes? In part, it is a question of generational artistic identity, as the same question (or sometimes accusation) frequently gets posed to Lethem contemporaries such as the filmmaker Quentin Tarantino, the visual artist Jean-Michel Basquiat, or any number of hip-hop artists whose entire art form is based on recontextualizing existing art. If Lethem is just recycling, then his work epitomizes some critics' sense that postmodern fiction proves that the well of literary inspiration has run dry. I argue instead that Lethem's particular interest in blurring the lines between literary fiction and genre fiction, and between the ephemerality of pop culture and the posterity of high art, offers opportunities for readers and critics to think about originality itself in new ways.

The focus in this book, though, is not on genre but on influence, which is an equally useful interpretive lens with which to approach Lethem's body of work. Lethem's major fiction and nonfiction approach in a variety of ways the question of what a contemporary writer, particularly one as well versed as Lethem in literary history and popular culture, is to do with the omnipresence of artistic influence. Lethem depicts a wide variety of uses to which his characters put the artworks they love: they can serve as binding forces between friends, valuable tools of identification as people create their own self-images, and markers of political commitment, among others. Certain questions about use (or in some people's view, overuse) of formative influences in contemporary literature remain, though. Does joyful appreciation of someone else's work—and desire to call one's own reader's attention to an influence's formative power—amount merely to standing on the shoulders of giants? Or might it result in rapturously new and unexpected originality, what Lethem has termed "the ecstasy of influence"? Questions of literary influence and originality have been fraught for decades, from Harold Bloom's influential poetic theory of the anxiety of influence, which largely dooms latecomer authors to pale imitation of their forebears, through John Barth's postmodern concept of the literatures of exhaustion and replenishment, which suggests that while latecomer authors may not have the tools to be original, they do have considerable tools of revision and redefinition. Lethem goes beyond even Barth's optimism, replacing the ennui of the writer born too late to be original with a vibrant excitement at the riches of the artistic archive. In effect, Lethem turns that archive from a burden to a playhouse, changing "it's all been done" into "look at all that's been done, and all that we can still do with it!" In doing so, he forces readers to redefine what originality means and to consider how much we should value originality anyway.

With this focus on influence in mind, this book examines the three Lethem novels that have received the most attention in academia and in the literary press thus far. *Motherless Brooklyn, The Fortress of Solitude,* and *Chronic City,* taken together, present a fairly cohesive picture of a contemporary American novelist coming to terms with both the joys and the downsides of artistic influence. *Motherless Brooklyn* works as both an homage to and a subversion of traditional hard-boiled detective novels as Lethem both accepts and questions the conventions of a genre he loves and by which he is influenced. Questions of personal aesthetics dominate *The Fortress of Solitude;* this novel dwells obsessively on appreciation and criticism of art, particularly pop music and comic books. Lethem's main character spends half a lifetime puzzling out the complexities of the art he loves, interrogating his own emotional and intellectual reactions to it, and thinking through the political implications of the ways he has been influenced by that which he consumes. *Chronic City* meditates on the cost of fandom and the potential dangers of giving over too much of oneself to the art that one loves most. It is less a repudiation of Lethem's earlier celebration of wild creativity than it is a fruitful mediation of that earlier implied position, dramatized via Lethem's first depiction of a character brought nearly to ruination not by the demands of artistic creation but by obsessive cultural consumption. Even before his landmark essay "The Ecstasy of Influence," Lethem has depicted characters who take great pleasure in appreciating and identifying with great art of the past. All the while he has written nonfiction that pays respectful and enthusiastic homage to the wide variety of artists—not only writers but filmmakers, actors, and musicians too—whose work has helped shape his taste as a consumer and his aesthetic as a creator of literary art.

In focusing on Lethem's later and relatively more mainstream fiction, I do not mean to critique negatively the early sci-fi novels through some kind of benign neglect or faint praise; in fact I will spend some time with a couple of early sci-fi stories that have received little critical comment thus far. Moreover, I agree with Lethem that to draw a sharp line separating "the fantastic" from "the realistic" in his work is to create a false dichotomy. Lethem has remarked about the critical category *magical realism,* "how I despise that term" (*Conv* 129), which he finds inherently patronizing. The category's existence and name, Lethem feels, say more about the literary critical establishment than they do about the substance of any fiction; literary realism is so frequently thought the default mode of respectable writers at this point that some new oxymoronic category now appears necessary to account fully for many notable writers' decisions to color outside the lines of strict mimesis.

Those boundaries do not apply to Lethem's fiction, which gleefully and promiscuously blends genres often thought incompatible. Any reader who comes to Lethem's early work for mind-bending sci-fi will also find the tenderly wrought coming-of-age of an adolescent girl in *Girl in Landscape* and a sharply funny academic satire in *As She Climbed across the Table.* Any reader who claims a preference for Lethem's alleged "realistic novels" must also embrace the presence of a magical invisibility ring in *Fortress* and a giant (possibly mechanical) tiger in *Chronic City.* Such elements strike some readers as virtuosic but disconnected from the emotional core of Lethem's fiction; for others, including myself, they are indispensable demonstrations of Lethem's viewpoint that fiction need not be constrained by verisimilitude to daily life. For that matter, such elements demonstrate his fiction's frequently recurring overarching tone of bemusement: a sense that all is not as it appears or as it ought to be.

For all of this book's interest in influence, I will not focus on this concept here to the exclusion of all other recurring concerns in Lethem's work. In addition to the formal interplay between realism and fantasy in Lethem's fiction, I also discuss how Lethem imagines cultural space (particularly the varied and always-morphing cultural spaces that make up New York City), his recurring use of dynamic duos and surrogate families, the racial politics of popular culture, and his quasi-sociological understanding of fandom and fan subcultures, among other topics.

That last item bears particular importance as a bridge between the idea of influence in the abstract and Lethem's peculiar set of notable allusions. Indeed, Lethem is an enthusiastic consumer of culture—highbrow, lowbrow, and all in between—and his work overflows with cultural references. A pop music sponge, a longtime reader of comic books, and a true cinephile, he incorporates frequent references to song lyrics, superheroes, and cult movies into his work, never doing so out of mere imitation or ironic homage (or worse, out of an off-puttingly transparent desire just to look cool) but out of recognition that cataloging one's cultural consumption actually can work beautifully as a mode of characterization or of constructing a literary setting. Since Lethem is so devoted to unearthing and reveling in his own influences within his work, the job of any critic writing about Lethem becomes in part to do some unearthing and revealing of those allusions and reference points. A reader of *Motherless Brooklyn,* for example, is well served by understanding how Raymond Chandler defined the hard-boiled detective novel as operating differently from previous mystery fiction. Full understanding of *The Fortress of Solitude* requires readers to grasp how an origin story operates within the form of the superhero comic. A couple of major plot lines in *Chronic City* owe much to the idea of the fatal title "entertainment" in David Foster Wallace's *Infinite Jest.* In other words, to explain fully the idea of influence *in* Lethem's work is to unearth and explicate fully the major influences *on* Lethem's work. If Lethem's work does indeed put readers into what one critic calls a "clue-reading habit,"[1] then a goal of this book is to illuminate those clues usefully in order to create a fuller, brighter picture of just what Lethem is up to.

Jonathan Lethem was born in Brooklyn, New York, in 1964, to Richard and Judith Lethem, a painter and a political activist, respectively. The Lethem family lived for a short period in the late 1960s in Kansas City, Missouri, where Richard Lethem taught at the Kansas City Art Institute; after a dispute with the school's administration over his activities in protest of the Vietnam War, the family returned to Brooklyn, to the neighborhood now known as Boerum Hill (*TDA* 88–90). Drawing from Lethem's book of autobiographical critical essays *The Disappointment Artist,* Evan Hughes compiles Lethem's descriptions of his parents in the late 1960s and early 1970s thusly: "His father was a serious and inventive painter, and his mother held odd jobs like piercing ears in Greenwich Village. She destroyed lettuce and grapes in the supermarket because they'd been picked by exploited migrant workers. Both parents were deeply involved in volunteering and liberal activism; they marched against Robert Moses freeways (one of which cut right through the neighborhood next door), against Vietnam, against nuclear power."[2] Lethem has recalled his mother letting him decide for himself what he should do when at age eleven he was offered marijuana for the first time (*TDA* 98). Pieces of this upbringing would inform Lethem's writing decades later in large ways and small. Lethem's interest in the gentrification of New York will drive *The Fortress of Solitude,* as his observations of how frequently staunch idealists fall short of their goals will appear in short stories such as "How We Got in Town and Out Again" and "Super Goat Man" as well as in his most recent novel, *Dissident Gardens.*

In returning to Brooklyn in the early 1970s, in a neighborhood where white families were in the minority, Lethem's parents were gentrifiers, Hughes allows, "but instead of being shut inside a claustrophobic house, the Lethems threw open the doors—to friends from back in Greenwich Village, to a new crowd from the area, even to other lovers. . . . The Lethems saw neighbors and potential allies in a new social order."[3] In addition Lethem's parents inform his depictions of some major characters in his later fiction: there are shades of Richard Lethem in Abraham Ebdus in *The Fortress of Solitude* and of Judith Lethem in Miriam Zimmer in *Dissident Gardens.* However, both characters are fictional and should not be taken as veiled representations of Lethem's parents. Lethem is not a writer of romans à clef.

As a child Lethem devoured books but harbored ambitions that were more in the visual than the literary arts. In an essay on Brooklyn's Hoyt-Schermerhorn subway station, Lethem recalls taking the New York City subway from that station to the High School of Music and Art, a Manhattan public high school, each day for four years. Since the trip was a full hour each way, allowing plenty of time for reading, Lethem claims that he "read five novels a week for the four years of high school" (*TDA* 49). Lethem has recalled that his reading was primarily classic sci-fi, which he says he read "like a machine, [but] I was much more selective—snobbish, even—about crime fiction. I discovered Hammett, Chandler, and Stanley Ellin, and decided nothing else was good enough. So I reread those guys obsessively" (*Conv* 35). It was no coincidence, then, that Lethem's first novel, *Gun, with Occasional Music,* wound up a sci-fi–inflected detective novel. As often as Lethem recalls his childhood reading as primarily genre fiction, though, a short reading list in his essay "The Beards" reveals just how broad the young Lethem's reading taste was: C. S. Lewis, J. R. R. Tolkien, Ray Bradbury, Kurt Vonnegut, Norman Mailer, Guy de Maupassant, Italo Calvino, Don DeLillo, Patricia Highsmith, and of course Philip K. Dick, the sci-fi writer for whose work he has most passionately advocated and whose influence Lethem readily claims (*TDA* 138–39). Influence is so important in Lethem's world that a short piece in *The Ecstasy of Influence* is devoted to what Lethem's *parents* read: John Updike, Tom Robbins, Marshall McLuhan, Timothy Leary, and Anaïs Nin, among others (*TEoI* 13–14). A similar catalog will appear in Lethem's fiction later, as the young Dylan Ebdus takes note of his mother's copies of Philip Roth's *Letting Go* and Henry Miller's *Tropic of Cancer* (*TFoS* 12).

Lethem's mother died of a brain tumor when Lethem was thirteen. In multiple interviews Lethem has suggested that all of his novels center on something that has been lost. In *Motherless Brooklyn* this is Lionel Essrog's surrogate father figure Frank Minna, murdered early in the novel. In *Fortress* this is Dylan Ebdus's mother Rachel, who leaves the family when Dylan is still a child. In *Chronic City* the central void may be the absence of Chase Insteadman's fiancée Janice, trapped in a space station, though given how frequently critics have begun to discuss *Chronic City* as a post-9/11 novel, this novel's driving loss may be more widely shared and totalizing than any loss shared by a single character. Lethem has written movingly of his mother in two essays in *The Disappointment Artist* in particular: "Lives of the Bohemians" and "The Beards." In the latter Lethem has marked time in the section headings by indicating the rough date of the anecdote described and then matter-of-factly labeling that date "mom dead," "mom undiagnosed," or the like.

After graduating from the High School of Music and Art, Lethem went on to Vermont's Bennington College, a liberal-arts school once known as the most expensive college in America. There he was classmates with fellow writers Bret Easton Ellis, Jill Eisenstadt, and Donna Tartt, though Lethem would not publish a novel until a decade after Ellis's debut. He dropped out of Bennington during his sophomore year but was invited back to give Bennington's 2005 commencement address. Indeed, in the introduction to Lethem's *Paris Review* interview in *Conversations with Jonathan Lethem,* Lorin Stein points out that among the generation of young male novelists with whom Lethem is frequently grouped—David Foster Wallace, Michael Chabon, Jonathan Franzen, Colson Whitehead, and others—Lethem is the only "inner-city kid" and the only one without a college degree (*Conv* 47). After leaving Vermont, Lethem spent the next decade in California, where he worked in used bookstores while he began publishing stories in science-fiction magazines and eventually novels. As fantastical as his early work could be, Lethem insists that autobiographical echoes remain visible. Even before writing *The Fortress of Solitude,* widely considered his novel that leans most autobiographically, Lethem discussed the sci-fi *Girl in Landscape* as an unlikely autobiographical novel. Before it becomes "a John Wayne Western on another planet," he explains, it is about "parentless adolescence in the neighborhood I grew up in" (*Conv* 31). Lethem moved back to Brooklyn in 1996 and began *Motherless Brooklyn,* the first of the three New York City–set novels on which this book focuses, all centered in some way on influence and passionate cultural consumption.

In the essay "Identifying with Your Parents" in *The Disappointment Artist,* Lethem describes his childhood attachment to the culture of his parents' generation as more intense than his interest in the art of his own time. Getting into David Bowie, for instance, as any number of children of the 1970s did, immediately sent the young Lethem investigating the work of Anthony Newley, the British actor-singer-songwriter to whom Bowie was sometimes compared early in his career. Lethem writes, "I suffered a kind of nerdish fever for authenticity and origins of all kinds, one which led me into some very strange cultural places. The notion of 'influence' compelled me, at irrational depths of my being. . . . So I was always moving backward through time, and though I was born in 1964 and came to cultural consciousness some time around 1970 or 1971, I particularly adored the culture of the fifties and early sixties: Ernie Kovacs, *The Twilight Zone,* the British Invasion, Lenny Bruce, the Beat writers, film noir, etc. I tended to identify with my parents' taste in things, and with the tastes of my parents' friends, more than with the supposed cultural tokens of my own generation" (*TDA* 63–64). How Lethem has manifested his interest in artistic influence throughout his career can be illustrated by how he has responded to a handful of major theorists of the concept of influence.

No discussion of literary influence and its theorists would be complete without dealing in some way with Harold Bloom's *The Anxiety of Influence* (1973), a landmark study of influence in English-language poetic history, though its arguments can be extrapolated to literature in other genres. Bloom's basic argument is that "strong poets" find ways to "misread" their predecessors in such a way that they throw off the weight of the literary masters who precede them. Influence "always proceeds by a misreading of the prior poet, an act of creative correction that is actually and necessarily a misinterpretation," Bloom claims, but he also frames good use of influence in terms of smart borrowing.[4] "Weaker talents idealize," he says; "figures of capable imagination appropriate for themselves."[5] Since its initial publication, *The Anxiety of Influence* has been discussed in critical circles in primarily Freudian terms: Bloom's assertion that strong poets must look for ways to overcome the influence of their ancestors has led many to view the book as something akin to Oedipal allegory. The artistically successful poet, this reading goes, must somehow kill the overbearingly dominant father. In a preface to the book's 1997 second edition, Bloom claims that he "never meant . . . a Freudian Oedipal rivalry, despite a rhetorical flourish or two in this book," explaining that "influence-anxiety does not so much concern the forerunner but rather is an anxiety achieved in and by the story, novel, play, poem, or essay. The anxiety may or may not be internalized by the later writer."[6] In other words, he understands the anxiety of influence to be not so much an emotional experience of the writer himself or herself as a textual feature of the work produced as a writer wrestles with his or her influences. "A poem is not an overcoming of anxiety, but is that anxiety," he explains.[7] While influence need not take the form of any single emotional or literary event, Bloom argues, all expressions of influence are "ultimately defensive in their nature."[8]

Furthermore, Bloom argues that strong writers must somehow work through and overcome their sense of their own belatedness: "Cultural belatedness is never acceptable to a major writer. . . . Belatedness seems to me not a historical condition at all, but one that belongs to the literary situation as such."[9] In other words, belatedness, like influence itself in Bloom's thought, is metaphorical. Belatedness is not the literal consequence of a writer's life span coming centuries after Shakespeare's or Milton's; instead it is the hallmark of a writer who becomes too caught up in his or her influences, too aware of following in the footsteps of literary achievement instead of discovering an original path toward one's own achievement. For Bloom, this is not an altogether positive proposition. On the one hand, being a latecomer remains for Bloom a near-inescapable burden. After complimenting the contemporary poets A. R. Ammons and John Ashbery, Bloom still detects "a strength that battles against the death of poetry, yet also the exhaustions of being a latecomer."[10] On the other hand, influence still gets cast largely in quite negative terms: "Everything that makes up this book . . . intends to be part of a unified meditation on the melancholy of the creative mind's desperate insistence upon priority."[11] Later he says that a "poem is a poet's melancholy at his lack of priority."[12] In a nutshell, that is the definition of influence that Lethem has spent an entire career rejecting. Lethem replaces Bloom's sense that most things worth writing have been written with an arms-wide-open appreciation that so many great things have been written and that they remain available to us readers as enjoyable aesthetic experiences and as sources of continued influence.

Put another way, consider how Lethem might respond to one more fragment of Bloom's definition of influence: "The young citizen of poetry . . . quests for an impossible object, as his precursor quested before him. That this quest encompasses necessarily the diminishment of poetry seems to me an inevitable realization, one that accurate literary history must sustain."[13] Here Bloom refers not only to the increasingly marginal cultural status of poetry as an art form but also to his a priori (and, his critics often counter, largely unsupported) claim that English Renaissance poetry is greater than that of the Enlightenment, which is in turn greater than that of the romantics, and so on as poetry diminishes in greatness through the ages of modernism and postmodernism. With Bloom so asserting the weight of a sacred literary past as irrefutably unshakable and unmatchable, what latecomer author would not view his artistic ancestors with some rancor? For one, Jonathan Lethem.

For further insight into just how Lethem goes about rejecting Bloom's vision in favor of a vision that allots more originality and creative freedom to the latecomer writer, consider John Barth, the postmodern novelist best known for conceptual fictions such as *Giles Goat-Boy* (1966) and the story collection

Lost in the Funhouse (1968). Barth's essay "The Literature of Exhaustion" (1967) makes the case that latecomer artists need not be demoralized over any sense that so many good plots have been printed and so many good characters already created. Instead this vast literary archive is waiting to be pillaged, as we have unprecedented ability to appropriate and reconfigure earlier texts. Barth defines exhaustion not as an ending but as an opportunity; it is "the used-upness of certain forms or exhaustion of certain possibilities—by no means necessarily a cause of despair."[14] Barth sees the artistic method of appropriation and recontextualization of past texts as a marker of genuine creativity, not as the end of the road of originality.

To illustrate this, Barth explains the conceit of the Jorge Luis Borges story "Pierre Menard, Author of the *Quixote,*" about a fictional writer who, circa 1900, having never read Cervantes's *Don Quixote,* writes several chapters of Cervantes's *Don Quixote.* Taking Borges, of whom he speaks glowingly, as inspiration (or one might say, influence), Barth imagines what else could happen should latecomer artists similarly reimagine the implications of earlier texts' appearing in the present, perhaps even under the names of other creators. With pop art's yen for re-creation as a valuable context, Barth explains, "if Beethoven's Sixth were composed today, it would be an embarrassment; but clearly it wouldn't be, necessarily, if done with ironic intent by a composer quite aware of where we've been and where we are. It would have then potentially, for better or worse, the kind of significance of Warhol's Campbell's Soup ads, the difference being that in the former case a work of art is being reproduced instead of a work of non-art, and the ironic comment would therefore be more directly on the genre and history of the art than on the state of the culture."[15] He goes on to enthuse, "What evenings we might spend (over beer) discussing [the modernist architect Eero] Saarinen's Parthenon, D. H. Lawrence's *Wuthering Heights,* or the Johnson Administration by Robert Rauschenberg!"[16] Though the specific artworks he is suggesting might well be ridiculous in reality, in concept Barth is serious. The idea here: reinterpretation of old ideas, plots, and characters may well be the best shot that a latecomer author has at doing something original. Barth was doing it already via his reuse of classical myth in multiple stories in *Lost in the Funhouse.* Also in the 1960s Barth published a faux eighteenth-century novel about a real eighteenth-century writer, Ebenezer Cooke, even poaching the title of Cooke's most famous poem for his own novel, *The Sot-Weed Factor* (1960). After all, he points out, the novel began in parodic celebration or critique of major authors' past influences: Cervantes imitating the romance and, in the eighteenth century, "Fielding parodying Richardson."[17] Barth's examples there give the lie to Bloom's assertion that major authors who imitate their influences are doomed to live in the shadows of earlier masters.

Thirteen years later Barth would revisit the ideas contained in "The Literature of Exhaustion" in a companion essay, "The Literature of Replenishment" (1980). In it he calls the earlier essay "much-misread," much as Bloom would later seek to clarify *The Anxiety of Influence.*[18] Barth reframes "The Literature of Exhaustion" by explaining that he did not mean to imply that he believed literature itself to be dead and finished in 1967, but instead that high modernism was dead and finished, a proclamation more about literary history than about literature itself and one that, in retrospect, sounds about right. He proposes in "The Literature of Replenishment" that the best thing contemporary postmodern fiction can do is seek to unite bourgeois realism and high modernist fragmentation. Where Barth's highest praise was earlier reserved for Borges, in the later essay he applauds the Italian novelist and short-story writer Italo Calvino, whose work Lethem knows well and about which he has written. Barth's descriptions of Calvino could also describe Lethem: his "materials are as modern as the new cosmology and as ancient as folktales, but [his] themes are love and loss, change and permanence, illusion and reality"; and he "grounds his flights in local, palpable detail," keeping "one foot in fantasy, one in objective reality."[19] Indeed, Lethem has pointed to Calvino as a guiding example: quite early in his career, he has recalled, he pulled together his varied influences and began imagining himself as "the American Calvino, but nourished by scruffy genre roots" (*Conv* 50).

Moving forward to Lethem's contemporaries, I suggest one writer and, even more specifically, one essay by that writer as helping shed further light on how Lethem views his literary ancestors. Michael Chabon was born less than a year before Lethem and, like Lethem, has published novels, short stories, and essays, all evincing a keen interest in the long traditions of genre fiction. Chabon's best-known work, the Pulitzer-winning novel *The Amazing Adventures of Kavalier & Clay* (2000), like Lethem's *Fortress,* looks to American superhero comics for both theme and content. Like Lethem's, Chabon's aesthetic with regard to influence eschews anxiety in favor of arms-wide-open appreciation. In "Fan Fictions," an insightful essay on the long literary life (via reuse and reappropriation) of Sherlock Holmes, Chabon asserts that "there is a degree to which . . . all literature, highbrow or low, from the *Aeneid* onward, is fan fiction. That is why Harold Bloom's notion of the anxiety of influence has always rung so hollow to me. Through parody and pastiche, allusion and homage, retelling and reimagining the stories that were told before us and that we have come of age loving—amateurs—we proceed, seeking out the blank places in the map that our favorite writers, in their greatness and negligence, have left for us, hoping to pass on to our own readers—should we be lucky enough to find any—some of the pleasure that we ourselves have taken in the stuff we love: to get in on the game."[20] In essence Chabon's explanation as to why he writes manages to reject Bloom explicitly while it embraces Barth implicitly. Chabon's essay maps out how writers coming after Arthur Conan Doyle have borrowed Holmes and Watson to fill out blank spaces in Holmes's world or to redress wrongs that they see in Doyle's vision of that world, which constitutes a clear culmination of Barth's vision of the possibilities of the literature of exhaustion. Chabon also explains that his goal as a writer is not to overcome his influences but to enter into meaningful conversation with them. To demonstrate this even more fully, Chabon imaginatively reinterprets an influence in the epigraph of *Maps of Legends,* the essay collection in which the Holmes essay appears. Chabon reproduces a brief and self-effacing comment about doing research on the whaling industry, which concludes, "I am transported with the reflection that I myself belong, though but subordinately, into so emblazoned a fraternity." Chabon cites the fragment "Herman Melville, on the writing of fan fiction." The Holmes essay concludes, "All novels are sequels; influence is bliss."[21]

"Influence is bliss" sounds quite a bit like the title of Lethem's own treatise on the positive value of influence, "The Ecstasy of Influence." But first, it is useful to map out what exactly Lethem has taken from each of these theorists. Almost all of the time Lethem appears to reject Bloom's agonistic perspective on literary influence. Asked in his *Paris Review* interview if he ever envies the successes of his contemporaries, Lethem demurs. "There are people who can do amazing things," he admits. "But I never take it personally. . . . You're not fighting the other writers—that Mailer boxing stuff seems silly to me. It's more like golf. You're not playing against the other people on the course. You're playing against yourself" (*Conv* 58). He disavows the combative poses of earlier writers, even of Norman Mailer, for whom Lethem has a soft spot. There is the rare moment, though the exception and not the rule, in which he speaks of influences from a prior generation in a slightly more adversarial way, though without going fully Bloomian. In discussing the genesis of *As She Climbed across the Table,* a novel whose academic setting and quasi-scientific jargon reflect the example of Don DeLillo's *White Noise,* Lethem recalls reading DeLillo with interest: DeLillo became "a crucial writer for me, an unavoidable writer, one whom I was going to have to digest and incorporate" (*Conv* 20). Indeed a minor Lethem work, the pseudonymous collaborative sports novel *Believeniks!* (2006), can be read as a nod to DeLillo's own pseudonymous collaborative sports novel, *Amazons* (1980), which Lethem has acknowledged knowing (*Conv* 108, *TEoI* xx).

Elsewhere, though, Lethem sounds far more Barthian, particularly when discussing *Girl in Landscape.* Lethem has spoken of this early sci-fi novel as an autobiographical work in seemingly unlikely ways, but he has also characterized it as a space-set rethinking of classic western plots. In particular he thinks of it as a retelling of the John Ford film *The Searchers* (itself the source plot for George Lucas's *Star Wars,* a favorite of the teenage Lethem, to speak of influence, not to mention Martin Scorsese's *Taxi Driver* as well) from the point of view of the teenage girl who is at the center of Ford's plot without ever being heard from terribly directly. "There's a generic postmodern move," Lethem explains, "an assault upon a classic work by taking the neglected or minority viewpoint and retelling the tale—think of Jean Rhys rewriting *Jane Eyre* as *Wide Sargasso Sea*. . . . It wasn't much of a leap to watch *The Searchers* and wonder about Natalie Wood's version of events. What might it be like to see John Wayne through her eyes? You can see how the idea fell to me very naturally" (*Conv* 55). It comes naturally, of course, only because Barth has called our attention to it in "The Literature of Exhaustion."

If Lethem sounds most like Bloom when discussing DeLillo, and if he sounds most like Barth when discussing his genre-bending tendencies, then he sounds most like Chabon when he discusses his vision for himself as a writer more generally. Asking himself the essential question of why he has chosen to make writing his life's work, he confides, "I began writing in order to arrive into the company of those whose company meant more to me than any other: the world of the books I'd found on shelves and begun to assemble on my own, and the people who'd written them, and the readers who cared as much as I did, if those existed" (*TEoI* 429–30). In these terms he appears to share with Chabon the conviction that all fiction is fan fiction, at least as far as all fiction writers begin their writing lives as passionate readers of fiction. For Lethem, this is not the cause of an anxiety to bemoan but a cause for celebration.

Lethem's own vision of the positive power of artistic influence is "The Ecstasy of Influence," a clever and highly conceptual essay that first appeared in *Harper's* in 2007 before becoming the title piece in Lethem's 2011 collection of (mostly) nonfiction. Heavily indebted to both Lawrence Lessig's *Free Culture* (2004), a landmark book in the nascent free-culture movement and a challenge to traditional notions of how American copyright law works, and Lewis Hyde's *The Gift* (1983), which posits the idea that art and artists are better served by a gift economy than a commodity-based one, "The Ecstasy of Influence" works as both a brilliant defense of creative appropriation and a call for a new, more generous understanding of copyright.

The essay attacks notoriously litigious holders of copyright, such as the Walt Disney Company and the J. D. Salinger estate, while praising artists, such as Bob Dylan, who borrow openly and extravagantly from those who have influenced them while also embracing the idea that their successors will borrow openly and extravagantly from them in turn. (Dylan, Lethem points out, "has never refused a request for a sample" [*TEoI* 105].) To marry form and content in this essay, Lethem pulls a clever trick: the bulk of the essay is itself creative borrowings from texts about creative borrowing, all of which are identified in a key at essay's end and none of which are identified as such in the essay itself. Before the key to the essay's borrowings, "The Ecstasy of Influence" runs about nineteen full pages as printed in the collection that shares the essay's title. If one maps out all of the borrowings laid out in the key, assumes that Lethem has composed the rest himself, and does the math to calculate how much of the essay then comes from Lethem's pen alone, that total comes to less than seven pages of the nineteen-page essay proper.

For all of the showy craftiness of the essay's guiding conceit, "The Ecstasy of Influence" proceeds from some quite serious opening questions. Lethem wonders why some people are still given pause by the accusations that Vladimir Nabokov may have lifted some plot elements of *Lolita* from an earlier German short story, while those same readers roll their eyes at the Margaret Mitchell estate for wanting to stop publication of Alice Randall's *The Wind Done Gone,* an audacious reframing of *Gone With the Wind* from an African American perspective. Or why the revelation of a debut novelist's lifting of passages wholesale from an earlier novel can result in a career stopped dead in its tracks, while no one cares at all when Bob Dylan lifts a few lines wholesale from the Confederate poet Henry Timrod and drops them into songs on the album *Modern Times.* Indeed, Randall's work, and arguably Dylan's, once again falls firmly in the tradition for which Barth advocates in "The Literature of Exhaustion." Lifelong Dylan fan that he is, Lethem explains elsewhere that he understands appropriation and originality to be much less mutually exclusive than many others would argue: "The kind of Bob Dylan paradigm was the one I believed in, that you could be the master thief and the originator and that those things were two sides of the same coin" (*Conv* 134). As he puts it in "The Ecstasy of Influence," "Literature has been in a plundered, fragmentary state for a long time" (*TEoI* 95).

The larger problem that writers now face, however, Lethem argues, lies less in critical or artistic communities and more in the public sphere: the very idea that creative appropriations such as Randall's or Dylan's might be considered legally actionable has chilling consequences not just for established artists such as Dylan but also, and more importantly, for emerging artists who may well do heretofore unimaginably creative things with past texts that might still be under copyright. In a section of the essay titled "The Beauty of Second Use," Lethem argues, "Artists and their surrogates [such as record labels, TV networks, movie studios, and literary estates] who fall into the trap of seeking recompense for every possible second use [of their earlier works] end up attacking their own best audience members for the crime of exalting and enshrining their work" (*TEoI* 104). There Lethem mounts a strong argument while connecting that tradition for which Barth advocates—strong writing that finds pathways to originality by recontextualizing the past—to that for which Chabon advocates—strong writing born out of good audience members' desires to enter into imagined and extended relationship with the texts that made them want to create. Lethem continues, "And artists, or their heirs, who fall into the trap of attacking the collagists and satirists and digital samplers of their work are attacking the next generation of creators for the crime of being influenced, for the crime of responding with the same mixture of intoxication, resentment, lust, and glee that characterizes all artistic successors" (104). Here Lethem defends his decision to wear his influences proudly on his sleeve and, with the word "successors," evinces no shame in being a latecomer to the creative party. He also opens his arms wide to artists who will come after him, positioning himself as the father who does not need killing in order for successors to thrive. True, with the word "resentment" he leaves open the possibility that artistic successors will respond negatively to their predecessors: consider, for instance, how many now-canonical texts by writers of ethnic minorities, particularly in the African American literary tradition, came out of a desire to redress the widely perceived misconceptions about minority peoples in earlier works. At the same time Lethem's emphasis on "intoxication" and "glee" points to his own joyful modus operandi and truly puts the "ecstasy" in ecstasy of influence.

Lethem also explains that too-vigilant defense of copyright can hinder the creative opportunities of artists coming from a position defined by a relative lack of privilege. An "enclosure of commonwealth culture for the benefit of a sole or corporate owner," he argues in a provocative comparison, "is close kin to what could be called *imperial plagiarism,* the free use of third-world or 'primitive' artworks and styles by more privileged" creators (*TEoI* 105). Lethem briefly invokes examples such as Paul Simon's controversial collaboration with black South African musicians during the apartheid era on *Graceland* or Led Zeppelin's uncredited borrowings of traditional blues songs, explaining, "Even without violating copyright, those creators have sometimes come in for a certain skepticism when the extent of their outsourcing became evident" (105). Lethem draws the comparison in order to emphasize that when large copyright-holding corporations get too possessive over the artworks they claim to own in full, they actually hinder the creative expression of individuals or of less wealthy organizations who lack corporate money or, perhaps more to the point, corporate legal representation.

Toward the end of the essay, Lethem makes a few bold and direct "assertions" that amount both to a clear summary of the point of view he defends in the essay and to a proposal for a more generous, less litigious vision of artistic appropriation that thinks of influence as a boon and not as a threat to creativity and originality. "Any text that has infiltrated the common mind to the extent of *Gone With the Wind* or *Lolita* or *Ulysses* inexorably joins the language of culture," he claims. "The authors and their heirs should consider the subsequent parodies, refractions, quotations, and revisions an honor, or at least the price of a rare success" (*TEoI* 110). There is Lethem's explanation of why Alice Randall ought to be celebrated (or at the very least allowed to publish *The Wind Done Gone* with minimal legal interference), while outright plagiarists who give no credit to their sources or actively seek to deceive are still worthy of our disdain. "Artists and writers," he continues, "too often subscribe to implicit claims of originality that do injury" to the idea, self-evident to Lethem, that all art is a collage of influence, memory, pure invention, and homage (112). He wraps up with a beautiful summary of what he expects from his readers: "Don't pirate my editions; do plunder my visions" (112). It is a useful and concise distinction between outright theft and artistic theft, bearing clear contempt for the former and generous respect for the latter.

As insightful and acclaimed as it is, "The Ecstasy of Influence" functions as much as a provocation as anything else, a valid and largely successful attempt to question whether the original utterance is still even possible. Some have expressed reservations about its effectiveness, while Lethem has acknowledged that, given its myriad borrowings, the essay's core claim is not 100 percent consistent: his own work "contradicted itself internally, as any rhetoric conflating file-sharing pirates and Thomas Jefferson were likely to have done" (*TEoI* 123). Zara Dinnen takes some issue with the essay's semblance of seamlessness, seeing it not as a dishonest act but as a missed opportunity. "Despite its hypertextuality," she asserts, "Lethem presents his essay to the reader as a closed object, proffering the illusion that it is self-contained."[22] Dinnen goes on to point out that when the essay appeared on the *Harper's* Web site, no hyperlinks were embedded in the text, which she suggests would have turned this "self-contained" text into a more radically open one. A truly hypertextual essay about originality, presented in a digital format, would broaden readers' experiences by enabling one to move quickly and directly from Lethem's thoughts about Lawrence Lessig's work to an excerpt of Lessig's work itself. Or at the level of sheer user-friendliness, hyperlinks could at least transport readers with a single click from the main text of the essay to the key and back, as e-books that use endnotes do quite easily.

Far more important than the essay's internal inconsistencies is its tone: Lethem celebrates the lack of originality in our artistic past instead of decrying it. Read in that spirit, the essay functions as a unifying force in exciting if paradoxical ways. Lethem acknowledges, and Dinnen agrees, that the pastiche text is hardly new. Once we have accepted that we are not original creators, Lethem suggests, we should all work on finding new and original ways to be unoriginal, and joyfully and creatively so at that. Even more usefully, Lethem has worked to originate a way to do just that. Lethem believes that when artists or their representatives monopolize the rights to adaptation of one's work, the "loser is the community, including living artists who might make splendid use of a healthy public domain" (*TEoI* 103). With that in mind, Lethem has created the "Promiscuous Materials" project, which offers to the public for adaptation some of his own previously published short stories (as well as the song lyrics of the fictional band in *You Don't Love Me Yet*) for a fee of only one dollar. Lethem's personal Web site includes a list of his work that is available for adaptation as well as a page of links to short films and audio files that have resulted from the project. Having reveled in influence and passionate consumption of others' creativity for an entire career, Lethem now offers some of his own work—more as a gift than as a commodity—for others to be influenced by in turn.

One other late essay is key to understanding Lethem's thoughts about the joy of the plentiful artistic archive. "Rushmore versus Abundance," which first appeared in *The Ecstasy of Influence,* argues that thinking about literature at any given moment in terms of Mount Rushmore–style generational pantheons of so-called Great Ones is inherently limiting. This is true not least of all, Lethem notes, because rarely, at least in the American critical tradition, do women or writers of color make those generational pantheons, which he summarizes as "Hemingway-Faulkner-Fitzgerald-Steinbeck," "Bellow-Mailer-Updike-Roth," "Heller-Kesey-Pynchon-Vonnegut," and "DeLillo-Coover-Barth" (*TEoI* 368). Contrasting our literary minds with our more limited consumers' minds ("supermarkets learn it's shrewd to make five premium mustards available, not twenty"), Lethem asks, "why should our grasp of literary culture, in its current state of explosive abundance and range, be hostage to this hindbrain's coping impulse?" (368). The idea here once again is that the abundance of available cultural production ought to be viewed as a boon to the creative mind, not as a burden.

Additionally, digital archiving and the current pop-cultural manias for reissues and nostalgia have given us unprecedented access to ever wider swaths of our cultural pasts, including high culture, low, and all that is in between. With such wide-ranging material available constantly, cultural consumers now have the ability to stay under the ecstasy of influence indefinitely. For Lethem, this is not entirely a bad thing, particularly as it gives every reader, viewer, or listener opportunities to explore both time-proven masterpieces and the boundaries of more idiosyncratic cultural interests. Responding to the accusation that the joy of appropriation contained in "The Ecstasy of Influence" represented an attack on the primacy and stability of the western canon, Lethem explained in a postscript to the essay that his love of past art requires the existence of a canon, but not a single canon dictated from on high. "I was a fiend for canons," Lethem affirms. "Let a million canons Bloom. Only, canons not by authoritarian fiat but out of urgent personal voyaging. Construct your own and wear it, an exoskeleton of many colors" (*TEoI* 124). There is a subtle but barbed pun there in Lethem's capitalization of "Bloom." Lethem invokes Harold Bloom again, in this case Bloom's *The Western Canon* (1995), a book whose appendixes include authoritative-seeming lists of all western texts that Bloom considers worthy of canonization. Bloom has claimed that the lists appear only at his publisher's insistence, but surely not every reader who takes Bloom's canon as authoritative knows that Bloom has insisted on the lists' contingency. If "The Ecstasy of Influence" is to be taken as mischief-making, as Lethem has suggested, its postscript ends with more mischief: invoking the idea of an authoritative canon, only to reject it immediately in favor of the oxymoronic but inviting idea of the individual canon.

In the early twenty-first century, cultural omnivorousness appears more the norm than ever. So many boundaries that once separated high culture from pop culture, chipped away at first by high modernism and then more so by postmodernism, have begun to break down that few bat an eye at even the oddest juxtapositions of others' eclectic tastes. Lethem rejects those old boundaries as he discusses his own taste: "I've never felt I had to pick from among *these* things and renounce *those others*. Good stuff's found across the spectrum. Boundaries aren't going to tell you where the good ones are; your interest, your Spidey-sense going off, is going to tell you" (*Conv* 57). In another interview he defines the term "literature" as "everything good that anyone's ever written. There's no other definition" (114). That said, Lethem is aware that science fiction has long been considered a lesser form in certain high-literary circles and that some sci-fi writers and readers want nothing to do with so-called literary fiction either. It would be inaccurate to assert that Lethem's move from publishing mostly in sci-fi magazines to his current status as a mainstream major novelist represents some intentional effort to transcend the literary ghetto in which science fiction has long existed. Instead, as Michael Kandel suggests, "it is simply that the ghetto walls do not exist for [him] and never did."[23] This idea comes through in particular in Lethem's frequent insistences that for all of the magical rings and miniature black holes in his fiction, his commitments to believable characterization, well-drawn settings, and effective plot structures actually make him more traditional than he gets credit for. In one interview he claims that his own "so-called originality—which is just as often called my 'surrealism' or my 'postmodernism' or what-have-you—tends to be overstated, at the expense of how deeply traditional my work is" (122). Of course, Lethem does not have in mind there what most people think of as "traditional" fiction—the well-made nineteenth-century realist novel and its descendants, created by the types of writer Barth refers to as "the technically old-fashioned artist."[24] He is defining tradition in terms of a kind of literary filial piety—simultaneous awareness that he is a latecomer and that is okay, that his own reading has created for him a virtual personal canon, and that his own work can operate within those traditions that he most regards.

More than any other writer of his generation, even Chabon, Lethem wears his influences on his sleeve. He is keen, he admits, "to spoil the illusion of originality by elucidating my fiction's resemblance to my book collection" (*TDA* 147). As he puts it elsewhere, "Before I began publishing, I'd imagined that pointing out my thefts would be the occupation of my enemies. I had no idea I'd be so routinely called to take up that work myself!" (*Conv* 54). His homages to other artists whom he respects tend to be more overt than covert. For example, take *The Ecstasy of Influence*—not the essay on influence, copyright, and originality, but the collection that shares the essay's title and contains over six dozen short pieces, many about film, visual art, music, and other literature. In comparing *The Ecstasy of Influence* (in form if not content) to Norman Mailer's mostly nonfiction miscellany *Advertisements for Myself* (1959), Lethem admits that at one point he wanted to title his own mostly nonfiction miscellany *Advertisements for Norman Mailer* (*TEoI* xxii). Other artists and works to whom Lethem pays tribute in the compendium of argument that is *The Ecstasy of Influence* include the television pioneer Ernie Kovacs; individual films such as Robert Altman's *McCabe and Mrs. Miller* and Nicolas Roeg's *Don't Look Now;* writers ranging from the expected J. G. Ballard, Roberto Bolano, and Shirley Jackson to the perhaps less expected G. K. Chesterton, Nathanael West, and James Agee; and musicians from Rick James to James Brown. Yes, Norman Mailer gets his own essay as well.

Two writers in particular who precede Lethem are essential to understanding Lethem's aesthetic: one Lethem has discussed in great detail and with great frequency; the other less so. Both value stories and forms that are intentionally, even aggressively marginal when compared to the broad middle ground of mainstream narrative storytelling, and both have seen their aesthetics trickle down to later writers who operate all over the creative map. The more frequently discussed in Lethem's body of work is the sci-fi novelist Philip K. Dick, while the less frequently discussed is the American film critic Manny Farber.

In high school Lethem read all the Philip K. Dick works he could get his hands on, later recalling that he had "taken the author into my body like wine and wafer" (*TEoI* 43). In his retelling, reading Dick is akin to communion in more ways than one. Lethem explains that in coming to understand Dick's work and in building relationships with a circle of fellow serious appreciators of the writer, Lethem gained a valuable understanding of how the alleged boundary separating sci-fi from literary fiction is perceived from both sides. In "Crazy Friend," an uncategorizable essay about Lethem's career-long efforts to draw attention and, for that matter, literary credibility to the body of work of Philip K. Dick, Lethem reveals "the structural resistance in the barrier I wanted to break down—resistance from both sides. My difficulty persuading writing teachers of the worth of my secret pantheon was only equaled by the shrug of most science-fiction people when I suggested DeLillo and Barthelme should interest them. . . . Unite the divided realms! But my private myth didn't translate" (33). During his years in California, Lethem got involved in the Philip K. Dick Society in its earliest stages of existence, beginning efforts at what he later termed "my gentrification campaign, that which culminates, twenty years on, with my chaperoning Dick into the Library of America" (49). Lethem edited three volumes of Dick's work for the prestigious Library of America series; taken together, these collections, released one each year from 2007 to 2009, include thirteen Dick novels. They also represent a very real posthumous canonization of Dick's life's work and, as such, a vindication that Lethem's convictions regarding Dick's greatness were well founded and that the lines separating sci-fi from the broader canon can be effectively blurred. Lethem also edited, with Pamela Jackson, *The Exegesis of Philip K. Dick* (2011), a nine-hundred-plus-page book of selections from Dick's journals and private writing, in which he describes visionary religious experiences.

Umberto Rossi has usefully detailed some of Lethem's more direct borrowings from Dick, particularly *Amnesia Moon*'s indebtedness to *Do Androids Dream of Electric Sheep?* and *Solar Lottery.* For all of the passion with which Lethem approaches Dick's work and legacy, and for all of the openness with which he admits to borrowing from Dick's aesthetic, Lethem's high esteem does not turn Dick into the untouchable ancestor, the strong writer whom the weak writer can only misread. "I never really looked at Philip K. Dick as a literary father," Lethem explains, but "more like a brilliant older brother whose brave and also half-assed forays charted wild paths for me to follow" (*TEoI* 66). Positioning Dick as a brother instead of a father or an ancestor may seem at first a small deviation from the usual metaphors with which we discuss influence, but it is a meaningful one. As much as Bloom claims that his theory of influence bears no intentional Oedipal echoes—that is, no poets killing their fathers, literally or not—Bloom does assert that only the very strongest writers can escape the shadows of the earlier greatness in which they live. If Lethem imagines Dick as his brother, then Bloom's anxiety summarily disappears. Plus, Lethem admits in "Crazy Friend" to having a Philip K. Dick–themed tattoo (51), so he cannot be imagining him as a figure too unapproachably sacred.

Also key to understanding Lethem's taste is Manny Farber's landmark essay "White Elephant Art vs. Termite Art" (1962), which has now influenced generations of film critics, viewers, and writers, Lethem among them. Widely considered among the most important American film critics, Farber championed filmmaking and filmmakers who seek not to announce their own importance (or as it were, self-importance) but instead dig deep into unexpected, less trafficked corridors of experience. In Lethem's explanation, Farber's essay "is a characteristically thrilling rhetorical gesture from a critic I adore" (*TEoI* 259).

For Farber, "white elephant art" announces its own momentousness and practically dares viewers to disagree. These films—sweeping biopics of presidents, epic historical dramas, adaptations of "Great Novels," and anything else that we might call "Oscar bait"—may look pretty, but the attractiveness of their surfaces forces them, in Farber's view, to sacrifice depth, particularly narrative and psychological depth. White elephant art also tends to be showy in predictable, acceptable fashions. "Termite art," conversely, has "no ambitions towards gilt culture."[25] It rarely if ever announces itself as a big deal, preferring instead to explore less familiar characters and paths, more interested in revealing a small slice of life in some detail rather than the broad but thin tapestry of white elephant art. Farber's distinction is at its clearest when he contrasts Michelangelo Antonioni's *La Notte* against Akira Kurosawa's *Ikiru*. On the one hand, Antonioni, a consummate white elephant artist, wants "to pin the viewer to the wall and slug him with wet towels of artiness and significance."[26] Kurosawa's film, on the other hand, makes much humbler use of "buglike immersion in a small area without point or aim, and, over all, concentration on nailing down one moment without glamorizing it, but forgetting this accomplishment as soon as it has been passed."[27] Lethem brings the contrast a few decades closer to the present and further crystallizes it via a contrast between "big, ungainly, awards-season stuff" and "prestige-immune routes of curiosity through the cultural woodwork" (*TEoI* xxi, xxii).

Farber and his distinction between white elephant art and termite art appear so central to Lethem's personal aesthetic that Lethem even applies the terms to his self-identity as a writer. Lethem casts himself as a termite writer as long as he is known for sci-fi work only, but he "clambered into a White Elephant suit" when he found greater and more mainstream success (*TEoI* 259). Surprisingly for Lethem, he then saw his opinions about matters literary or otherwise taken more seriously, best summarized in an anecdote about how a desultory negative remark about Colin Powell while on a book tour in Europe became headline news in Italy overnight (259).

Lethem places himself clearly on the side of termite art, even going so far as to imaginatively request a specific piece of termite art: in a short piece collected in *The Ecstasy of Influence,* he imagines a fourth chapter of Francis Ford Coppola's *Godfather* series that would "forsake any impulse toward [white elephant art concepts such as] *the epic* or *the broad-canvas pageant of history*" in favor of burrowing even more deeply into crevices of the familiar story. "Show us a Korean War scene," Lethem suggests, wondering, "just how did Michael earn his medals? Give us Fredo's life in Vegas. . . . The cannoli—when and by whom were they eaten? Who *baked* the cannoli?" (*TEoI* 163; italics in original). It is as clear a rejection of white elephant art values in favor of termite art values as any Lethem has produced. His characters often do the same: Perkus Tooth in *Chronic City* in particular champions expression that is well off the beaten path, so much so that when he takes interest late in that novel in a piece of fairly mainstream comedic filmmaking (oddly, Steve Martin's 1982 neo-noir pastiche *Dead Men Don't Wear Plaid*), we are meant to understand this shift in taste as a much more totalizing shift in character. Even a novel of comparatively panoramic scope such as *The Fortress of Solitude,* telling the stories of multiple entire lives lived in multiple boroughs and, later, multiple coasts, tends to reveal its characters' deepest selves in their smallest gestures and subtlest nuances of cultural consumption.

On a few occasions Lethem's homages to his influences take the form of quick shout-outs, small references that casual readers may not even notice. For example, a radio station in *You Don't Love Me Yet* is named KPKD in brief tribute to Philip K. Dick's initials—a reference not instantly obvious but hardly hidden or occult either. On the other end of the spectrum is a truly obscure reference in *As She Climbed across the Table,* as the novel's narrator compares his romantic rival to his own "personal Stanley Toothbrush" (45). Toothbrush is the title character of a 1962 story by the American sci-fi writer Terry Carr. When Lethem's editor objected to the reference, rightly noting its obscurity, Lethem responded, "That's for me. Just leave it there" (*Conv* 16); Toothbrush gets one more brief mention in the middle of *Chronic City* as well (*CC* 251). Before moving on to the major novels, though, I linger here on a few early short stories that reveal how Lethem's references to his influences can be far more complex than those quick drive-by allusions as well as how often he speaks to the unusual situation of the latecomer artist.

Lethem's respectful homages to his literary ancestors can be surprisingly totalizing and inherent to their works' meanings, seeking to recontextualize the earlier narrative touchstone entirely. Lethem's most direct application of this idea in his own work comes in the short story "How We Got in Town and Out Again," which first appeared in *Isaac Asimov's Science Fiction Magazine* in 1996 and later, in 2006, became half of the two-story volume *How We Got Insipid*. The story borrows wholesale much of the premise and plot of Horace McCoy's 1935 novel *They Shoot Horses, Don't They?*, right down to Lethem's female main character sharing the first name Gloria with McCoy's protagonist. The McCoy novel depicts a Depression-era dance marathon in which destitute people compete desperately in a grueling weeks-long endurance competition and gradually become aware that they are being treated cruelly, like sideshow performers who exist only to entertain an affluent crowd of spectators. Lethem's story replaces the dance marathon, however, with a contest to see which of several competitors can remain in a virtual reality environment the longest. In some ways Lethem's story is far more optimistic than McCoy's novel—at the very least, Gloria makes it out of Lethem's work alive, unlike McCoy's—but Lethem has cast his story as "a slashing attack on the utopian assumptions surrounding the promotion of what was then called virtual reality" (*How We Got Insipid* 106–7). He borrows McCoy in order to critique a particular kind of 1990s hyperoptimism about technology. Along similar lines is the very early story "Ad Man," first published in *Science Fiction Review* in 1992 and eventually incorporated into "Crazy Friend," the long essay on Philip K. Dick. In it a serious-minded painter finds his work infiltrated by invisible robotic microprocessors that turn his artwork into advertisements for soft drinks. Lethem has placed "How We Got in Town and Out Again" in a long lineage within the long history of sci-fi as well: he has called it a late entry in the tradition in which "the skeptical 1950s-style science fiction writer takes a debunking position on his society's infatuation with technological development, usually in light of some instinctively Marxist sense of how capitalism corrupts the reception of radical technology" (*Conv* 7). It is precisely the sort of thing Barth imagined in "The Literature of Exhaustion": a transparent and intentional reuse of elements of a recognizable literary text of the past in order to make specific and trenchant comments about the present. For that matter, the other story in *How We Got Insipid*, "Insipid Profession," parodies Robert Heinlein's "The Impossible Profession of Jonathan Hoag," resulting in a two-story collection defined by creative appropriation.

Another key early Lethem story also anticipates in vital ways what will become career-long concerns in Lethem's body of work. Collected in *The Wall of the Sky, the Wall of the Eye*, "Vanilla Dunk" is about the racial politics of popular culture every bit as much as the more overtly political *The Fortress of Solitude* is, but it also focuses on the expressive difficulties peculiar to the latecomer postmodern artist. Curiously, Lethem has called it "my normative story, my attempt to show I can keep you just as enthralled with completely innocuous, uncontroversial material" (*Conv* 12). That is true only to the point that "Vanilla Dunk" is less emotionally intense than other early stories of his—most notably "The Happy Man," also collected in *The Wall of the Sky*—but that is not to say that this story does not also depict controversial action while entering into existing aesthetic controversies regarding the fate of the latecomer creative type.

The story takes place in a future-world NBA in which drafted players take part in a lottery through which they are assigned the "subroutines"—that is, the skills, playing styles, and general athletic personae—of past basketball greats, whose skills become eligible for reassignment fifteen years after their original retirements. Players wear those skill sets during game play via "exosuits," though Bo Lassner, the story's narrator, admits to turning his exosuit off at times since his natural jump shot is better than his subroutine's. As the story begins, Michael Jordan's subroutine, the most desirable possible for obvious reasons, is up for grabs, and it winds up going to a hotshot named Alan Gornan, who is brash, young, and, not least of all, white. Gornan christens himself "Vanilla Dunk" at his postdraft press conference, and when the narrator, a teammate of Gornan, sees this display, he instantly compares Gornan's "sneer" to "pictures I've seen of the young Elvis Presley" (*The Wall of the Sky* 75). Lethem's implication is clear: Gornan is about to make a load of money and court a load of controversy as a white guy performing African American style. Soon Gornan will infuriate teammates with his explanation of his self-proclaimed nickname. "Vanilla," he claims, is "completely smooth and completely sweet" and "a breath of fresh air," while chocolate has "always got that bitter edge" (85). The less-than-flattering racial undertones of the comment are obvious.

Lethem is far too savvy about the centuries of fruitful racial cross-pollinations of American culture, however, to dismiss immediately Gornan's actions as mere minstrelsy. His real problem, Lethem implies, is not his use of black performance practices, but the unthinking crassness with which he appropriates them. In contrast, Lassner—also a white player using the exosuit representative of a retired black player—comes to Gornan's defense with an angry teammate more thoughtfully. "You're sampling, I'm sampling. This isn't some purist thing, man. Get some perspective," he insists, invoking the language of hip-hop's primary creative modus operandi and, arguably, the primary creative currency of all postmodern art (*The Wall of the Sky* 81). To clarify it yet more fully (if a bit clunkily), he continues, "Basketball is postmodern now" (83).

As such, the story also reflects smartly on the condition of the latecomer artist. Take this description of the story's future-world pro basketball landscape: "The supply of old NBA stars was pretty much depleted. It was only a couple of years after Jordan retired that the exosuits took over, and basketball stopped growing, started feeding on itself instead" (*The Wall of the Sky* 70). Replace basketballers with literary novelists, and the passage now looks like any number of common critiques of postmodern metafiction: it is self-consciously, paralyzingly late to the creative party; it reuses past greatness instead of innovating; and it is too smugly and self-awarely clever to do much but chase its own tail.

Perhaps surprisingly, though, the story shifts from being primarily concerned with racialized performance to being primarily concerned with postmodernity, even after a dramatic moment in which Gornan calls a black opponent "nigger" during a game. Lethem does not make this incident the story's climax, however, indicating that while race is consistently in play in his work as a core concern, that concern is only one of many. The story becomes most fully about the latecomer creator after a trade that results in Lassner becoming an opponent of Gornan. Elwood, a new teammate as well as the target of Gornan's on-court epithet, tampers with Lassner's exosuit altogether without Lassner's knowledge, admitting, "I just noticed you play better without it, man" (*The Wall of the Sky,* 101). After their new team wins a championship, Elwood credits Lassner with having "taught himself to play without sampling [since] the skills they gave him sucked" (116). He emphasizes metaphorically that originality remains possible to the truly great artist. After insisting that his team beat Gornan and not Jordan for the win, Elwood utters "a strangely heartfelt jumble of sports clichés" that Lassner sees as undeniably genuine (116). He calls him "the last modernist in a sport gone completely postmodern" (116), equating sincerity and emotion with modernity, and the artificial and cold with postmodernity.

For those postmodernist critics amenable to Fredric Jameson's contention that late capitalism turns even the most innovative cultural products into mere commodities, it is worth noting that in Lethem's future NBA, teams are named for corporations, not cities. Of course, Lethem is also thinking here in the same mode as those tech-skeptic sci-fi writers whom he invokes in discussing "How We Got in Town and Out Again" and whom he casts as often working from Marxist assumptions. Gornan plays for the Gulf and Western Knicks as the story begins (*The Wall of the Sky* 70). Additionally, after Gornan's Knicks lose to Lassner and the Disney Heat, Gornan practically becomes a multinational corporation by giving up basketball and signing with United Artists Tokyo to make movies and records. He concludes that all such enterprises are "just entertainment" and, I would add, ultimately commodities (118). If Lethem's future NBA in "Vanilla Dunk" is negatively postmodern, it is not because it is a place where originality is impossible or undesirable or because all innovation winds up commodified. It is because it is overly weighed down by the ghosts of past greats and overly concerned with rearranging pieces of the past instead of creating anew.

By having Bo Lassner find his greatest success only after turning off his exosuit in "Vanilla Dunk," Lethem argues that originality is still available to the artist who seeks it and values it. The three chapters ahead argue that, taken together, Lethem's three major New York–set novels, all quite original books in their own ways, depict in turn the value of celebrating the art that one loves and by which one is influenced, the joys and the dangers of intellectualizing or overinterpreting that art and influence, and the potential pitfalls of identifying with that art too passionately and solipsistically. Additionally each of these three novels features a highly reflective protagonist who spends much of the respective book trying to figure out how to make sense of an unusual personal past. These reflections on the characters' attitudes toward the past wind up including, by extension, reflections on aesthetic experiences that have influenced these characters in their respective youths or provided opportunities to identify imaginatively with elements of their cultural consumption. In other words, just as Lethem seeks to articulate a useful role for influence in the aesthetic of the latecomer writer, so his characters seek to articulate a useful role for that culture that they consume and that shapes them and their worldviews.

Lethem does not ever entirely turn off his exosuit, so to speak, in any of these three novels: they are filled with references big and small to the art and literature that have influenced him and made him want to produce literature, and I see part of my job here as the explicator of those references. Never let it be said, however, that Lethem's approach to creative appropriation and reuse of those materials that so influence him amount to merely unoriginal borrowing or pastiche. True, literary fiction may be as unavoidably sample-based and influence-heavy as Bo Lassner's future NBA. By no means, however, does that turn influence into an idea or an experience that is easy to make sense of. Lethem, after all, has spent a career meditating on influence and originality.

CHAPTER 2

Motherless Brooklyn

Self-Aware Influence and Stylized Genre

Lethem's early science fiction works are genre novels, but rarely are they novels about the idea of any particular genre itself. In other words, while his sci-fi bears unmistakable imprints of influence, especially from Philip K. Dick, he does not often write about the idea of science fiction itself. That is not the case with *Motherless Brooklyn* (1999), Lethem's breakthrough novel and a book as much *about* hard-boiled detective fiction as it is a hard-boiled novel in its own right. *Motherless Brooklyn* won the 1999 National Book Critics Circle Award for fiction, Lethem's first major mainstream literary award, and many critics recommend it as the best introduction to Lethem's style and recurrent concerns. It is also unusual in that it is Lethem's first novel that fits clearly within a traditional category of genre fiction without seeking to blur the lines between multiple types of genre fiction. *Amnesia Moon,* for instance, is part post-apocalyptic tale, part road novel. *As She Climbed across the Table* works both as a straight romance and as a bit more uncategorizable piece of DeLilloesque speculative scientific paranoia, and *Girl in Landscape* is half interplanetary sci-fi and half western with a healthy dash of adolescent coming-of-age drama. *Motherless Brooklyn,* conversely, is a detective novel, which, James Peacock asserts, "becomes remarkable when one considers the novels that preceded it, all of which brought multiple genres rudely into collision."[1] Lethem's comments on the novel seek to complicate things a bit, though. He dismisses the idea of *Motherless Brooklyn* as noir, calling it "just a crime novel" while also admitting the possibility that it is "a Bildungsroman, a family romance, a coming-of-age story, whatever. It's also a 'geek' novel, in the tradition of *Catcher in the Rye* and *A Confederacy of Dunces*" (*Conv* 35–36). While Lethem's other suggestions have some validity, the fact remains that *Motherless Brooklyn* is full of direct invocations of the American hard-boiled fiction masters Dashiell Hammett and Raymond Chandler, while direct invocations of J. D. Salinger or John Kennedy Toole are nowhere to be seen.

American hard-boiled detective fiction, as perfected by the likes of Hammett and Chandler and further popularized in any number of film noir works about steely private eyes and saucy femmes fatale, is marked by two important tonal qualities. At least in its primary male (anti-)heroes and narrators, controlled, often baroquely metaphorical language and emotional coolness recur. For the latter, recall any number of classic Humphrey Bogart lines: Rick's "I stick my neck out for no man" in Michael Curtiz's *Casablanca* or Sam Spade's "When a man's partner is killed, he's supposed to do something about it. It doesn't make any difference what you thought of him" in John Huston's *The Maltese Falcon,* the latter based on a Dashiell Hammett novel that is a key intertext for *Motherless Brooklyn.* Lethem complicates the familiar noir mood and tone immediately, in introducing *Motherless Brooklyn*'s narrator and protagonist, Lionel Essrog, by highlighting his Tourette's syndrome. It is hard for a detective to remain coolly restrained, both emotionally and linguistically, when he lives with a condition that places both his language and his self-presentation outside of his own control.

If there is a single text that can serve as a kind of rule book for the hard-boiled novelist, it is undoubtedly Raymond Chandler's essay "The Simple Art of Murder" (1944). Though Lethem has never referred directly to this particular Chandler essay, he has acknowledged that "taking on [the detective novelist and Lew Archer creator Ross] Macdonald and Chandler as prose models is how I taught myself to write" (*Conv* 160). Chandler's essay explains how hard-boiled fiction differs or, perhaps more accurately, ought to differ from more polite and traditional detective fiction, particularly the genteel English country-house mystery novel, most popularized by Agatha Christie. In its insistence on a reasonable level of verisimilitude in even the most genre-defined fiction, it resembles Mark Twain's classic debunking of early nineteenth-century adventure novels, "Fenimore Cooper's Literary Offences" (1895). Chandler opens, in fact, by stating, "Fiction in any form has always intended to be realistic."[2] Just as Twain patiently explains away all that is illogical in a few scenes of Cooper, Chandler provides a numbered list of seven major plot holes in a once well-regarded detective novel called *The Red House Mystery* by A. A. Milne, best known as the creator of Winnie-the-Pooh.[3]

In contrast, Chandler speaks approvingly of his contemporary Hammett, best known for *The Maltese Falcon* (1930) and *The Thin Man* (1934). Hammett, Chandler argues, brought a streetwise and naturalistic American energy to a novelistic form that "because of its heavy crust of English gentility and American pseudo-gentility, was pretty hard to get moving."[4] Chandler continues his critique of the overly polite detective novel by casting it as far too genteel for its own good: "Hammett took murder out of the Venetian vase and dropped it into the alley; it doesn't have to stay there forever, but it was a good idea to begin by getting as far as possible from Emily Post's idea of how a well-bred debutante gnaws a chicken wing."[5] Above all, he explains, a piece of detective fiction becomes invalid if a murder occurs in it primarily for the purpose of setting a plot in motion because, well, a detective novel needs a corpse. Instead hard-boiled fiction depicts a world in which people sometimes kill other people out of believable motives, grounded in convincing characterizations of people who live in recognizable places.

Of course *Motherless Brooklyn* is far too individual a novel—with its Tourettic narrator, its hard-nosed Brooklynite resentment of Manhattan, and its unusually intricate plotting—to follow all of the rules that Chandler sets out. Yet a comparison of *Motherless Brooklyn* with another short Chandler text, the essay "Twelve Notes on the Mystery Story," reveals numerous affinities. First, it is worth noting that Chandler's essay, unpublished in his lifetime, can be read as a direct rejoinder to the "Ten Commandments" of detective fiction created by the English novelist Ronald Knox, a writer of just the sort of heavily plotted, genteel fiction that Chandler so disdained. In actuality Chandler agrees with Knox more than he disagrees, though Chandler's dismissal of fanciful devices such as "fantastic poisons" or "snakes climbing bellropes"[6] would likely lead him to quibble with Knox's claim that a single secret passage—but just one—is allowable. That said, Chandler's numbered prescriptions again value the realistic plot over the mechanical plot and narrative logic over mere atmospheric romance.

Lethem puts this aesthetic to use in such a way that his work approaches its predecessors with more of an air of generous celebration than agonistic competition. Since Lethem largely follows Chandler's rules in *Motherless Brooklyn,* the novel becomes an excellent exercise in accepting the weight of literary history without being visibly burdened by it. Put another way, Lethem's reuse of Chandler's aesthetic rules does not smack of Bloom-like anxiety or intentional misreading of the predecessor; nor should this novel then be read as a Barth-like exercise in the literature of exhaustion that merely borrows and resituates existing literary material. If anything in the range of theories of influence summarized in chapter 1, *Motherless Brooklyn* becomes a Chabon-like example of purely joyful quasi-fan fiction. Lethem revels in the possibilities and the limitations of genre fiction alike—faithfully executing some characteristics of hard-boiled fiction while gleefully questioning and ignoring others—while depicting a character (the detective with Tourette's syndrome) and a setting (gentrifying Brooklyn) that Chandler and Hammett could not have imagined. The noir mode of American genre writing and dramatic film of the 1940s and 1950s, Lethem has explained, is not defined in his mind by a stereotypical mood and emotional tenor symbolized by cigarette smoke, shadows, and lonely saxophones in the distance. Instead it is all about "vibrant, hostile, punning, impossible language" and "tremendous narrative disjunctions," all of which he can retain while jettisoning some of hard-boiled fiction's more familiar features (*Conv* 34). Lethem cites writers not associated with hard-boiled fiction as key influences on *Motherless Brooklyn* as well. "Stylistically, I was thinking of the masters of New York slang, like Ring Lardner, and more recently, Richard Price, people who deal energetically with New York's street language," he explains, including Don DeLillo in his novel *Libra,* depicting a preassassination Lee Harvey Oswald in the Bronx (107).

Furthermore, Lethem had been genre bending for his entire career, and his debut novel in particular sought to meld hard-boiled fiction to a wider range of genre influences. Lethem has described *Gun, with Occasional Music* as "a piece of carpentry [in that] I wanted to locate the exact midpoint between Dick and Chandler" (*Conv* 51). This novel's epigraph is a quotation from Chandler's late novel *Playback* (1958): "There was nothing to it. The *Super Chief* was on time, as it almost always is, and the subject was as easy to spot as a kangaroo in a dinner jacket." Less than sixty pages in, Lethem introduces an antagonist for our detective hero Conrad Metcalf: an "evolved kangaroo . . . wearing a canvas jacket" (*Gun, with Occasional Music* 57). Here, Lethem takes the traditionally baroque hard-boiled simile of the Chandler epigraph and literalizes it. It is comparable to any number of *New Yorker*–style humor pieces that start with an untenably odd premise or fact, often a piece of decontextualized found language from a police blotter or news story, quoted as an epigraph and brought to a comically logical end in the main text. *Gun, with Occasional Music* ought not be read as a straight detective story either, and not only because of its elements of the fantastic such as the talking kangaroo. John Garrison's persuasive Marxist reading of that novel posits the partial replacement of language with music in the world of the text as a tool of sociopolitical control.

Motherless Brooklyn is difficult to summarize, and as is the case with a great deal of hard-boiled fiction, the ins and outs of the intricate plot are not necessarily the point of the book. Indeed, as Jennifer L. Fleissner has put it in asserting that the novel is as much about Lionel's language as anything else, "As with many a shaggy-dog detective story, one tends to forget the supposed 'main narrative' of *Motherless Brooklyn* in the intervals between rereadings. Who killed Minna again? Why did they do it? These puzzles are generic ones;

the text achieves its distinctiveness, by contrast, in its proliferation of Lionel's verbal tics."[7] I would agree; while the reader's continued desire to have unanswered questions answered does keep one turning pages, this novel is ultimately an idiosyncratic character study that also works quite hard to invoke a particular vision of New York City. Indeed, Chandler acknowledges in "The Simple Art of Murder" that few readers of Hammett's *The Maltese Falcon* ever really concern themselves with the question of who killed Sam Spade's partner Miles Archer—"the only formal problem of the story."[8]

As in classic hard-boiled fiction, character, setting, and atmospherics of language and genre dominate here, but plot still matters. With that in mind, to summarize: Lionel Essrog is a teenaged orphan who, along with a few other residents of St. Vincent's Home for Boys named Gilbert, Tony, and Danny, is taken in by Frank Minna, a streetwise small-time crook in Brooklyn. Minna puts his young charges to work helping him move stolen property while deftly keeping them basically unaware of exactly what they are doing. All the while Lionel's coworkers become a surrogate family of sorts—the "Minna Men," he consistently calls them—as Lionel looks up to Minna as a protector and mentor. For his own part, Minna calls Lionel "Freakshow" for much of the book, reacting to Lionel's Tourette's with equal parts amusement, condescension, and confusion. Eventually, in early adulthood, the Minna Men run a detective agency that fronts as a taxi service. As the novel opens, Minna has just been killed, and Lionel attempts to investigate the murder, feeling considerable grief over the death of his surrogate father and considerable guilt for not being able to stop the murder, as Lionel had been trailing Minna through Manhattan in another car. Readers eventually discover that Minna was killed by a hired gun representing a large Japanese corporation from which Minna and his brother Gerard had been stealthily embezzling funds. This revelation occurs only after Lionel has come into contact with a pair of small-time Old Brooklyn organized crime bosses, investigated a Buddhist zendo (where he meets a love interest of sorts), and followed all of these leads all the way out of New York City to coastal Maine, where Lionel puts it all together in a conversation with Frank Minna's widow.

Lionel describes his Tourette's syndrome as making all of his attempts at speech aberrations, but not necessarily in negative ways. In the novel's first paragraph, Lionel narrates, "I'm a carnival barker, an auctioneer, a downtown performance artist, a speaker in tongues, a senator drunk on filibuster" (*MB* 1). His speech gets cast as unusual, but not lesser communication than so-called normal speech. Still, his difficulties with language cause genuine internal psychic tension, as implied in his later comparison of Tourette's to a "seizure of language" (175). As Lionel starts trying to develop relationships with the other

Minna Men, attempting to play everything as cool as would the streetwise young man he would like to be, "a sea of language was reaching full boil" at the same time (46). All the while, though, both Lethem and Lionel understand that his garbled language can be entertaining: Lionel recalls that Minna "adored my echolalia. He thought I was doing impressions" (57). Indeed the barrages of mangled words that flow from Lionel's mouth often come across less as Lethem exploiting a character's disability and more as surrealist flights of linguistic fancy. In the novel's opening pages, a verbal tic is set off in Lionel after he notices that the building he and Gil are staking out is a Buddhist zendo. Instantly, Lionel's "brain was busy," he narrates, "with at least some low-level version of echolalia salad: *Don't know from Zendo, Ken-like Zung Fu, Feng Shui master, Fungo bastard, Zen masturbation, Eat me!*" (4). Later an attempt to call Tony "dickweed" during an argument will devolve into a helpless utterance of "Restrictaweed, detectorwood, vindictaphone" (78). When Lionel hears the name Alfred Hitchcock, he explains, he "silently replie[s] 'Altered Houseclock' or 'Ilford Hotchkiss'" (46). His own name, for that matter, is "the original verbal taffy," as it can shift from Lionel Essrog to "Liable Guesscog," "Final Escrow," or "Ironic Pissclam" (7).

For all of the unfamiliarity inherent in the unusual language of Lionel's narration, Lethem also has Lionel work to normalize his Tourette's syndrome by suggesting how his obsessions, tics, and verbal manglings ought to be more familiar to readers than they might first admit. Lionel's fanciful imagined band names for the Minna Men, such as "Jerks from Nowhere" and "Free Human Freakshow" (*MB* 64), are echolalic imitations of Minna's own language for his followers that could also pass for real band names. After awkwardly waving to the doorman of a building he is investigating, Lionel is surprised to see the doorman wave back, only to conclude that "everyone's a little ticcish that way sometimes" (160). Most notably, Lethem has Lionel cast New York as "a Tourettic city" after seeing lines of New Yorkers buy lottery tickets (and instantly lose) at a newsstand. Lionel watches their actions and concludes that "this great communal scratching and counting and tearing [of lottery tickets] is a definite symptom" of Tourette's (113). The image of the Tourettic city extends underground: Lionel asserts, "There is nothing Tourettic about the New York City subways" (192), only to revise his opinion rather comically forty-five pages later: "On second thought, there is a vaguely Tourettic aspect to the New York City subway, especially late at night—that dance of attention, of stray gazes, in which every rider must engage. And there's a lot of stuff you shouldn't touch in the subway" (237).

As much as the casual reader may be tempted to agree with Minna anytime he calls Lionel "Freakshow," Lionel offers frequent reminders of how regularly everyone engages in nervous, tongue-tied, or "ticcish" behavior—and how sometimes such behavior can be worked to a detective's advantage, as Lionel makes his ever-present obsessive vigilance into an observational asset or occasionally uses his idiosyncrasies strategically to lower others' expectations of him as an investigator. Ultimately, as Peacock puts it, "one of the pleasures of the story is the revelation that Tourette's is, in fact, perfectly suited to detective work."[9] Lionel admits early on that the other Minna Men "loved doing stakeouts with me, since my compulsiveness forced me to eyeball the site or mark in question every thirty seconds or so," summarily making those stakeouts easier on Lionel's partners (*MB* 4). As a result of his surprising aptitude at investigation, Lionel finds in the Minna Men one of the many surrogate families for a lost soul in Lethem's fiction. Coming from an orphanage as did the rest of the agency's detectives, Lionel has no family he knows, and quite early he notes that the Minna Men had "begun to function as a team" (50). He still feels bereft of deeper connections, though. In an unusually poignant scene, Lionel sees that there are few enough other Essrogs in the New York phone book that he could try calling them all. He begins doing just that, creating "a ritual out of dialing their numbers and hanging up after a tic or two, or listening, just long enough to hear another Essrog breathe" (69). Soon thereafter, when Minna has all of the boys to his mother's place for Christmas dinner, he tells her, "I got all of motherless Brooklyn up here for you. Merry Christmas" (71). The gesture is simultaneously warm and dismissive: it reminds Lionel and his friends just how unmoored they really are while offering some temporary but real holiday solace. Meanwhile, as Lionel navigates high school, he remains frustratingly (for him) undefined by any prepackaged group identity. In other moments he describes his Tourette's as less burdensome, but as a teenager he finds it isolating. "I wasn't tough, provocative, stylish, self-destructive, sexy, wasn't babbling some secret countercultural tongue," he explains. "I was merely crazy" (84). The Minna Men provide the best chance he seems to have at belonging.

Until, that is, Minna's murder gives Lionel an opportunity to join imaginatively the long tradition of streetwise big-city detectives, and crucially, Lethem gets a chance to bring his detective-novel influences into the pages of *Motherless Brooklyn* in ways both subtle and overt. At first, though, this tradition's fictionality makes no apparent difference to Lionel, as he plays the part of the hard-boiled private eye from the novel's first page—initially unknowingly but with increasingly sardonic self-awareness as the story progresses. The first glimpses of Lionel's hard-boiled pose come through via his yen for figurative language. Hard-boiled fiction makes frequent use of delightfully unexpected, sometimes quite baroque metaphors and similes. To borrow briefly from Chandler again, the opening paragraph of *The Lady in the Lake* (1943) compares a shop display of perfume bottles to "little girls at a dancing class."[10] A drunk who appears early in *The Long Goodbye* (1953) "snore[s] like a grampus" when asleep and has "eyes [that] were like holes poked in a snowbank" when awake.[11]

Lethem sprinkles such descriptive (if sometimes unnecessarily complicated) comparisons liberally throughout Lionel's narration, initially in order to convey the disorder Lionel feels in his own mind. In the novel's first paragraph, Lionel describes the rush of words from a Tourettic brain as disruptive but harmless, "tickling reality like fingers on piano keys" and akin to "an invisible army on a peacekeeping mission; a peaceable horde" in that they are ever present but also easy to ignore (*MB* 1). A bit later, when he involuntarily fixates on a corny joke about a talking piece of string, Lionel says that his mind "had shackled itself to the string joke like an ecological terrorist to a tree-crushing bulldozer" (32). The uncontrollability of his own actions reappears when, at the unremarkable sight of a woman passing on the street, Lionel cannot stop himself from whipping his head around to watch her, "my actions as exaggerated and secondhand as a marionette's" (73). Late in the novel, Lethem introduces a useful new coinage for Lionel to use in describing his inherent contradictions: "I'm tightly wound. I'm a loose cannon . . . they should be one word, tightloose" (261, 262). Then the metaphors return as he compares himself to "an air bag in a dashboard . . . all I do is compress and release, over and over" (262). At other moments, though, Lethem opts for unusual turns of phrase instead of complex similes. This happens particularly in describing the more prosaic work of the investigator's life, to unexpectedly atmospheric effect. My favorite is a quick phrasing that occurs when Lionel, while at home, sneaks a quick peek out his window to see if a policeman has trailed him back to his apartment. Instead of describing the street as bare or the coast as clear, Lionel notes, "The corner was empty of cop" (117).

In small moments Lethem casts Lionel and the rest of the Minna Men as quintessential noir characters. Physically they are stereotypical heavies: "oversize, undereducated, vibrant with hostility even with tear streaks all over our beefy faces" (*MB* 35). The homicide detective who questions Lionel after Frank's murder is a stock character too, "with his 10 P.M. Styrofoam cup of coffee, worn tie, ingrown beard, and interrogation eyes" (106). Much later a bravura paragraph that seems lifted straight from a film noir romance, part of Lionel's only close-to-real romantic encounter in the novel, contains a line that one could easily imagine Bogie saying of Bacall: "I'd never before kissed a woman without having had a few drinks. And I'd never kissed a woman who hadn't had a few herself" (220).

In a wide variety of other moments, however, the stuff of hard-boiled fiction gets gleefully poked fun at or rejected. Frank Minna finds ridiculous Gilbert's use of the term "piece" in place of the simpler word "gun" (*MB* 8), rejecting slangy pop-detective lingo. Later, Tony will call Lionel "Marlowe" in derision, invoking Chandler's fictional hero as the ideal detective whose example Lionel could never match (178). He goes on to dismiss Lionel as comparable not even to one of the Hardy Boys, seeing him rather as a "Hardly Boy," and he ends the tirade by comparing Lionel to McGruff, the cartoon canine cop of 1980s commercials, and, at best, "Shitlock Holmes" (179). When Lionel begins investigating the Buddhist zendo for its connections to Minna's murder, he imagines himself approaching the building as "that black outline of a man in a coat, ready suspicious eyes above his collar, shoulders hunched, moving toward conflict," invoking at the very least the stereotypical profile of the perfectly successful private eye (226). Lionel recognizes the stock characterization as such but goes on to explain that in actuality, while he may be "that same coloring-book outline of a man," in his case that outline has been scrawled by an insane or mentally challenged child (226). More often than not, when Lionel subverts his own ability to solve crimes, he does so via direct reference to his Tourette's. Occasionally, though, he measures himself against the noir hero and finds himself lacking in experience or nerve. Having previously taken over 130 pages to realize that he might be a detective, he takes over twice as long to reveal that he has never fired a gun (281).

To a certain point, deviations from the usual hard-boiled playbook are even more pronounced when Lionel goes home, to an apartment above the storefront where Minna's alleged taxi service has set up shop. Lionel describes his attempts at drawing some separation between work and home first in terms that can pass for Tourettic obsessiveness: he has different drinks of choice upstairs and downstairs, a preference for cards at work and chess at home, and so on (*MB* 116). More telling, though, is the loving detail with which Lionel has furnished the space, "decorating the apartment conventionally with forties-style furniture from the decrepit discount showrooms" (*MB* 116). He has chosen a modern touch-tone phone for downstairs and "a Bakelite dial phone" for his apartment, presumably for nostalgic value (*MB* 116). The space is exactingly planned to help support a private fantasy. It does not have a decorator (not that Lionel could afford one), but it has a production designer; there are no knickknacks, given Lionel's "faux-Japanese simplicity" (*MB* 117), but there are props. Even his drinking habits are performative, as he explains that he does not particularly enjoy his Johnnie Walker Red (an appropriately lower-end scotch for the small-time detective), but "the ritual was essential" (*MB* 117). Lethem has remarked of Lionel in his seminatural habitat, "The illusion that he's a Chandler character is only sustainable in the theatrical set of his own apartment" (*Conv* 39). Knowing as we do that Lionel read voraciously as a child and still does—there are Salvation Army paperbacks in that apartment too—it stands to reason that Lionel has some self-awareness about this self-created persona.

In fact by novel's end Lionel emerges as surprisingly self-aware about his own existence within a story reminiscent of hard-boiled fiction, without ever fully crossing over into the self-aware territory of high postmodern fiction in which literary characters know their own fictionality. For a book that is so grounded in a specific place, frequently rendered with a gritty (if stylized) naturalism, *Motherless Brooklyn* is full of direct references to detective fiction as both idea and institution—both as Lethem's formative reading and his present literary influence. While the earliest pages of *Motherless Brooklyn* reveal Lionel's infatuation with excessively hard-boiled language in his narration, he will soon move into more thoroughly performative territory, remaking himself as a heroic noir detective. A remarkable paragraph of Lionel's narration reveals how completely he attempts to cast his own identity in the image of a Philip Marlowe or a Sam Spade: "Minna Men wear suits. Minna Men drive cars. Minna Men listen to tapped lines. Minna Men stand behind Minna, hands in their pockets, looking menacing. Minna Men carry money. Minna Men collect money. Minna Men don't ask questions. Minna Men answer phones. Minna men pick up packages. Minna Men are clean-shaven. Minna Men follow instructions. Minna Men try to be like Minna, but Minna is dead" (*MB* 90). Lionel clearly is performing the received standard role of "private detective," filtered through Chandler, Hammett, and Bogart. Everything in the paragraph's description of the ideal Minna Man is exterior: appearance and action, with no room for interiority or actual lived individual identity. Try as he might, though, however totalizing this identity becomes for Lionel, it does not blot out of his mind a very real, if sublimated, grief following Frank's murder.

Even his perceived failures will wind up being recast in his own mind, on occasion, as merely performed failures akin to his performative apartment and drinking habits. While attempting to ingratiate himself to a woman connected to the mysterious Buddhist zendo at the core of the novel's mystery, Lionel notes, "My words came out thickened and stupid, like those of a defeated boxer in his dressing room, or a Method actor's, while playing a defeated boxer" (*MB* 207). On one level it is just a typically baroque hard-boiled simile. While one can only wonder whether Lionel has anyone in particular in mind (Brando in *On the Waterfront*? Montgomery Clift in *From Here to Eternity*?), he is still understanding his own role in his own investigation to be not fully real, not fully make-believe, and quite definitely mediated by moody American films from decades ago. Moments such as these lead Lethem to assert that even if the novel does not say so explicitly, Lionel clearly knows his Raymond Chandler too. “It didn’t follow that someone like Lionel could be so explicit and generous with his cultural references and so extensive in this cultural vocabulary and yet be oblivious to the references that would be most germane to him and his own aspirations,” he notes. “Why would someone like him want to be like him *unless* he’d read Raymond Chandler?” (*Conv* 88).

One entire paragraph on Lionel’s burgeoning self-awareness is worth reproducing in full, largely because it contains a direct address to the reader. After finding out that a mysterious potential lead named Ullman has been killed before he has had any chance to meet or question him, Lionel remarks, “Have you ever felt, in the course of reading a detective novel, a guilty thrill of relief at having a character murdered before he can step onto the page and burden you with his actual existence? Detective stories always have too many characters anyway. And characters mentioned early on but never sighted, just lingering offstage, take on an awful portentous quality. Better to have them gone” (*MB* 119). Lethem does not have Lionel admit to his own fictionality here, but he does let Lionel continue to understand Ullman as a plot device, more MacGuffin than human. Lionel owns up to feeling some small sadness about the death simply because “my clue had been murdered” (119). A couple of chapters later, it begins to dawn on Lionel that he has become “Minna’s successor and avenger,” another in a long line of Brooklyn tough guys, though now one with a peculiar purpose (132). He suddenly but warily concludes, “It seemed possible I was a detective on a case.” In what might be Lethem’s single most clever subversion of the hard-boiled tradition, he has his main character realize for himself with the sudden force of revelation that he is in fact a detective—132 pages into the novel.

Not surprisingly, then, Lionel continues to mediate his acts of investigation through his experiences of pop detectives, with whom he now finds himself identifying. Later, when he is trapped in a car full of heavies, put on the defensive as he is forced to make a secret-seeming cell phone call in their presence, Lionel starts to realize that his perceived control of the situation is slipping away. While talking on the phone, he pantomimes “a just-wait signal to them, hoping they’d recall the protocol from crime movies: pretend they weren’t there listening, and thus gather information on the sly” (*MB* 149). The genius and danger in Lionel’s move there is that he assumes (successfully) that his antagonists are just as susceptible to influence from familiar genre conventions as he is. He immediately recognizes one of the heavies as “schooled enough in the clichés to be manipulable” (149). Still, that is not to say that everyone with whom Lionel comes in contact accepts the conventional detective image so readily or expects to see it in real life. Near the novel’s end, while driving through Massachusetts on the way to the small coastal Maine town where the novel's plot threads will get resolved, Lionel speaks with Kimmery, his contact from the mysterious Buddhist zendo, insisting, "I'm a detective." She responds, "You keep saying that, but I don't know. . . . I thought detectives were more, uh, subtle," to which Lionel replies, "Maybe you're thinking of detectives in movies or on television. . . . On TV they're all the same. Real detectives are as unalike as fingerprints, or snowflakes" (255). Lionel understands here that the cliché is just that; he identifies himself as operating outside of the cliché (as his Tourette's syndrome requires) but realizes that careful invocation of the cliché is a smart move in the dangerous world he inhabits. The blurring of lines here between real detective and TV detective means that the archetypal detective becomes less an idea to which Lionel must aspire and more a tool he can pull from the detective's toolbox when he needs to control a contact who seems controllable.

As pervasive as the idealized figure of the classic hard-boiled detective is within *Motherless Brooklyn,* though, Lethem makes sure not to let that stereotype float unmoored from its origins. Indeed this novel invokes classics of hard-boiled fiction rather directly. In so doing, Lethem gets to wear his influences on his sleeve while Lionel gets to appeal to the fictional characters who serve as his models for how to perform the role of detective. Just over halfway through the novel, Lionel has a standoff with Tony, another Minna Man, who insists that Lionel did not mean near as much to Frank Minna as Lionel would like to believe. "You're the jerk I've gotta deal with," Tony, with gun in hand, snaps at Lionel. "You're Sam Spade." Lionel's response is both poetically appropriate and a slick literary appropriation. "When someone kills your partner you're supposed to do something about it," he replies (*MB* 183). While not quite verbatim, the line is a direct lift from the final pages of Dashiell Hammett's *The Maltese Falcon* (1930), a bit of dialogue re-created fairly faithfully in the John Huston–directed 1941 film adaptation starring Humphrey Bogart. In this classic of American hard-boiled fiction, Sam Spade has just informed his client Brigid O'Shaughnessy that his partner Miles Archer, killed early in the plot, "was a son of a bitch" whom Spade cared little for and intended to fire soon anyway.[12] He goes on to explain that "when one of your organization gets killed it's bad business to let the killer get away with it."[13] While Lionel would like to think that his relationship with Frank Minna meant more than Spade's with Archer, Tony plants doubt in his mind, cruelly comparing Minna and Lionel to a telethon-hosting "Jerry Lewis [and] the thing in the wheelchair" (183). As the standoff continues, Lionel returns the argument to the more familiar territory of hard-boiled narrative. When Tony insists that Lionel's only knowledge about the world comes from books and Minna, Lionel implicates Tony, asserting a shared love of and influence by genre fictions: "Everything we both know comes from Frank Minna or gangster movies" (194). Even as their conversation gets less specifically couched in reference to *The Maltese Falcon,* Tony cannot escape the cinematic language: on the next page he accuses Lionel of long-windedness by asking whether "every conversation with you [has] to be the director's cut" (185).

Chandler gets his moments of direct homage via quotation in *Motherless Brooklyn* as well. Lethem includes direct quotations of *The Big Sleep* twice, in quotation marks and attributed to Philip Marlowe (*MB* 205, 307). The second of the two direct Chandler quotations precedes an assertion about the detective genre from Lionel that casts him as a self-aware (and astute) reader of hard-boiled fiction. He notes that "in detective stories things are always *always,* the detective casting his exhausted gaze over the corrupted permanence of everything and thrilling you with his sweetly savage generalizations. . . . Seen it before, will see it again" (307). In addition to turning himself into a fashionably exhausted been-there-done-that, seen-it-all detached noir hero, Lionel uses this observation to explain how his mode of interacting with the world is fundamentally Tourettic. Generalizations are "a version of Tourette's," he says, because they are a way of "touching the world" and "covering it with confirming language" (307). In other words, just as Lionel will paint his city of residence as the most appropriately Tourettic one and his favorite musician as the most appropriately Tourettic one, so he has been describing his occupation, the detective, as the most appropriately Tourettic one. Of course he has been telling us this since the novel's opening, bragging a bit about how he is the Minna Men's most valuable private eye at stakeouts.

Lethem's range of reference points in *Motherless Brooklyn* is not limited to the literary. As in nearly all of his fiction but particularly in these three major New York–set novels, comments on characters' consumption and use of pop texts comprise vital layers of detail about how these characters live and view the world. At their least complex, these allusions can function as quick punch lines; at their most complex, they reveal the lasting influence of formative aesthetic experiences. In the novel's first page Lionel explains which Dick Tracy villain he would be, if forced to equate himself with one (*MB* 1). In the Upper East Side instead of Court Street, Brooklyn, the Minna Men are like the tiny playing pieces in a Monopoly game, inexplicably transferred to Candy Land or the mansion from Clue (3). In the second page he describes his corralling his tics not in terms of chaos and control but of "Kaos and Control," referring to the warring espionage units in the 1960s sitcom *Get Smart* (2). Television references abound as Lionel recalls not seeing anyone like him on TV as a rerun-watching kid (37), though later he is aware that the high-school-aged misfit Minna Men "looked like rejects from *Welcome Back, Kotter*" (86). Lethem the cinephile makes use of classic film references too: Frank Minna wears a "Robert-Ryan-in-*Wild-Bunch* grimace" (6). Minna accuses Tony of trying to act like Al Pacino in *Scarface* and later tries to explain how surveillance works in detective work by unsuccessfully invoking Francis Ford Coppola's *The Conversation* (76). But most importantly, Lionel again describes looking to film in attempts at identification with visible people whose tics and obsessiveness he shares. He finds these moments of identification in silent film, as he compares his own "overwound" body to "a production line like the one in *Modern Times,*" noticing how Charlie Chaplin along with Buster Keaton were "blazing with aggression, [and with] disruptive energies barely contained, they'd managed to keep their traps shut, and so had endlessly skirted danger and been regarded as cute" (47). Chaplin becomes, in a small but vital way, an influence on Lionel, if not as prominently so as Chandler.

Among all of the other pop material with which Lethem engages in *Motherless Brooklyn,* pop music is a vital presence, not as central to this novel as it will be to *Fortress* but employed for some key purposes of characterization. Lethem uses a character's musical taste to introduce the idea of racial division into the novel. One of the orphans-turned-Minna-Men, Danny, gets described as "a ringer [who] only looked white" and "had assimilated to the majority population at St. Vincent's happily, effortlessly" (*MB* 42–43). That said, Lionel points out that his listening habits tend toward funk and early hip-hop: he "listened to Funkadelic and Cameo and Zapp and was as quick to embrace rap as any boy at the home," putting him in a curious "suspension, neither black nor white" (43). Lionel's cultural consumption differs from Danny's: he claims that he practically "grew up in the library of St. Vincent's Home for Boys" and "set out to read every book" there (36, 37). Yet Lionel also recalls reading Booth Tarkington in that very library, sounding the words half aloud to the rhythm of the Sugarhill Gang's seminal single "Rapper's Delight," and beginning to realize that if there is other rhythmic, surreal, fancifully imaginative language around, he can use it to make sense of more orderly language (46). The quick reference to this record here prefigures the crucial scene of the teenage Dylan dancing with white friends to "Rapper's Delight" in *Fortress.* Similarly the idea, epitomized here in the reference to Danny's taste, that musical preferences function as surprisingly complex racial identity markers will become a core theme of *Fortress.*

If there is a single scene that functions as the musical heart and soul of *Motherless Brooklyn,* however, it is no doubt Lionel's page-long ode to the music of Prince and its Tourettic qualities. He explains that the first piece of music that took on deep personal meaning for him was Prince's 1986 single "Kiss," a sparse, jerky, minimalist funk tune sung almost entirely in (sometimes strained) falsetto. That meaning comes entirely out of what Lionel sees as the song's Tourette's-like ticcishness. "To that point in my life I might have once or twice heard music that toyed with feelings of claustrophobic discomfort and expulsive release . . . but here was a song that lived entirely in that territory, guitar and voice twitching and throbbing within obsessively delineated bounds, alternately silent and plosive," goes Lionel's rather accurate description (*MB* 127). Lionel buys the single on cassette, and better yet, he winds up owning not the radio edit he first heard but an extended mix "with a four-minute catastrophe of chopping, grunting, hissing and slapping sounds appended—a coda apparently designed as a private message of confirmation to my delighted Tourette's brain" (128). He begins to think of Prince as a therapeutically secret partner in ticcish crime: Lionel sees himself as "exempt from my symptoms" when listening to Prince and compares his music to "the nearest thing in art to my condition" (128). He finds in this music a Tourettic compatriot, not unlike the inspiration he takes from *Mad* magazine cartoonist Don Martin, who also receives a page-long tribute (222–24), that he will never find in the Minna Men.

Furthermore, Lionel turns this act of listening to what he calls "my brain's balm" into something that fulfills primal, even carnal desires. It has the same effect on him as sex or food, he explains, as "Prince's music calmed me as much as masturbation or a cheeseburger" (*MB* 128). The latter half of that comparison is no small thing in a novel that, as Peacock has pointed out,[14] has an appropriately obsessive interest in cataloging and describing in loving detail the food that Lionel enjoys. This scene is also representative of a type of moment that, starting with *Motherless Brooklyn,* begins to appear more and more frequently in Lethem's fiction: the moment of reflection on a particular (often pop-) cultural artifact in a way that does not advance plot at all. Lethem begins allowing these detours more space in his novels, and in one interview he compared *Motherless Brooklyn* to his earlier sci-fi work, which had comparatively little room for these sorts of lyrical digressions: "I was always in a terrible hurry. At some level I thought it was illegal for an 'inventive' writer to dally over real information. It took Essrog, with his obsessiveness, to stop and talk about Prince or a turkey sandwich with Russian dressing for a full page" (*Conv* 55). Perhaps inevitably, that very obsessiveness brings about one of the novel's best comic asides.

The idiosyncratic ticcishness of Lionel's language and speech lead him to multiple attempts at pronouncing the cryptic symbol that Prince took as his stage name for most of the 1990s. On one page Lionel verbalizes it as "Skrubble" and "Plavshk"; a page later it has become "Skursvshe" or maybe "Plinvstk" (*MB* 113–14). Humor aside, the moment also reveals how Lionel attempts to order the world: if Tourette's causes Lionel to produce some occasionally mangled language, Lionel will at least attempt to put whatever mangled language he has to a use as appropriate as possible in making sense of the world's oddities, however small. It is the same principle as reading Tarkington to a hip-hop beat, just in reverse: he reads stable, organized language on a page with the help of imaginatively odd oral language, and he uses imaginatively odd oral language to help explain something printed that seems unexplainable.

Equally unexplainable to Lionel at times is the complex cultural space that is New York City. Much of Lionel's thought and observations about New York (particularly the title borough) in *Motherless Brooklyn* will reappear in the narration of *The Fortress of Solitude,* also set in Brooklyn. The novel is set in the 1990s, amid the continued gentrification of Brooklyn that dates back to the 1970s setting of the opening chapters of *Fortress.* Lionel places his remembrances of the orphanage in which he grew up in "the part of downtown Brooklyn no developer yet wishes to claim for some upscale, renovated neighborhood; not quite Brooklyn Heights, nor Cobble Hill, not even Boerum Hill" (*MB* 36). The latter is the neighborhood, once called Gowanus but rebranded with its newly aspirational and vaguely Dutch name, in which Dylan Ebdus will grow up in *Fortress.* A more fully gentrified neighborhood gets depicted early in Lionel's working relationship with Minna, as the Minna Men meet some shady-seeming business associates of Minna's (whose role in the novel's complex plot will be made clear only at the book's end). Lionel describes the area as simultaneously old and new, uneasily mixing the durability of classic New York brownstones with the disposability of quick new developments: "some canny salesman had ten or twenty years before sold the entire block on defacing these hundred-year-old buildings with flimsy tin awnings over the elegant front doors," he narrates (59). Inside, "the front room's old architecture was intact. Through the single door we stepped into a perfectly elegant, lavishly fitted brownstone parlor. . . . It was more like a museum diorama of Old Brooklyn than a contemporary room" (61). The apparent identity crisis attached to the cultural space that is contemporary New York will be further explored in *Chronic City.*

In *Motherless Brooklyn,* suffice it to say that Lionel and the other Minna Men appear to have internalized an inferiority complex that threatens to doom Brooklyn to perpetual living in Manhattan's shadow. For Lionel, at least, this occurs because he imagines his first home to be not Brooklyn, and not even the St. Vincent's orphanage, but the orphanage's library. Every bit the voracious reader as the young Lethem, Lionel still casts his childhood reading in terms of failure because he finds no "signs of my odd dawning self" in the St. Vincent's library (*MB* 37). He credits Minna with helping him find a place in the world—"it was Minna who brought me the language, Minna and Court Street that let me speak" (37)—but until that point, Brooklyn is not so much a bad place as it is no place at all, a nonplace. It is significant, then, that one way Minna brings

Lionel more fully out into the world is by giving him a book, one called *Understanding Tourette's Syndrome.* As brusque as Minna's presentation of the book is, as he tells Lionel, "Turns out you're not the only freak in the show" (81), Lionel takes the book as a real gift, revealing that this is the first time he has ever realized that his condition has a name. While the book does not entirely normalize Tourette's in Lionel's mind, it does have the effect of making him feel less fully alone, which in turn enables him to begin to engage with a broader world.

That world is initially limited, though, and, in Lionel's observation, consistently looked down on by others. Brooklyn is "the ancient, battered borough [that] was officially Nowhere, a place strenuously ignored in passing through to Somewhere Else" (*MB* 37). Much later Kimmery, Lionel's contact from the zendo, will say of the zendo's roshi, "He isn't from *Brooklyn*. He's a very important man." Lionel instantly retorts in his narration, "She made it sound as if the two were mutually exclusive" (216; italics in original). In adulthood Lionel is capable of conveying that dismissiveness to the reader, but he says nothing to Kimmery directly about her contempt for his borough.

As will later be the case in *The Fortress of Solitude,* where one goes to school in New York bears particular baggage (or conversely, cultural capital). Lionel's fellow St. Vincent's resident Tony has a brief stint at the private Brooklyn Friends School, thanks to the generosity of a foster family. It does not last long, as he is found in bed with his foster parents' daughter, but even this short view of a more privileged world grants Tony respect from Lionel. It hardly matters that all Tony reports finding at Brooklyn Friends are cute girls and easy basketball opponents (*MB* 39–40). Lionel later describes Sarah J. Hale, his high school (and in *Fortress* the high school Mingus attends), as "a required stop except for those few who'd qualified for some special (i.e., Manhattan) destination, Stuyvesant or Music and Art" (*MB* 54). Lethem attended Music and Art, and Dylan Ebdus in *Fortress* goes to Stuyvesant. In comparison, Lionel appears to have fully internalized the inferiority complex he images Brooklyn to bear in the face of Manhattan. That said, he finds another surrogate family within Hale, where kids from the orphanage look out for each other: "Black or white, we policed one another like siblings," Lionel reports (*MB* 54). At any rate, he is at least more charitable than Arthur Lomb in *Fortress,* who compares Sarah J. Hale to prison and winds up going elsewhere after his mom falsifies their address on some paperwork *(TFoS* 126, 223).

Lionel's apparent chip on his shoulder about the bum rap Brooklyn gets in comparison to Manhattan appears to come out of his own fear of the big world outside of his borough, though. He speaks of non-Brooklyn New York in fearful terms, emphasizing his discomfort with elaborate mysteries such as this novel's plot and basic social interaction: he has "something to fear from the skyline, the big world of conspiracies and doormen that was Manhattan" (*MB* 208). He is not alone in this, though. When Frank's widow Julia explains to Lionel that she is about to leave town entirely, she asks him pointedly but not unkindly, "Have you ever been out of New York City?" (105). Lionel's silence answers for him, as she continues, "Because if you had, you'd know that anywhere else is a place of peace" (105). On his drive to Maine, where Lionel finds all the information he needs, he implicitly answers Julia's question while driving through Connecticut, noting that he is now "farther out of New York City than I'd ever been" (251).

In adulthood Lionel simultaneously fetishizes Manhattan as desirable and aspirational and weighs down Brooklyn with every possible association of authenticity and underdog grit, just as Dylan Ebdus will do in *Fortress.* While on the stakeout that opens the novel and ends with Minna's murder, Lionel takes note of "the orderly street life of the Upper East Side," admiring the area not for its affluence but for its relative lack of ticcishness (*MB* 9). While traveling across the Brooklyn-Queens Expressway, Lionel takes the opportunity to cast Manhattan as untouchable, a place to be yearned for: "Like the G train, the BQE suffered from low self-esteem, never going into citadel Manhattan, never tasting the glory" (25). Brooklyn, for its part, gets cast as idyllic, but only within certain boundaries that Lionel defines, borrowing heavily from Minna's view of the world. "Minna's Court Street was the old Brooklyn," he explains, a place where prices had not gone up in years, under-the-table betting still took place, and above all, "people looked out," Lionel adds with conspiratorial ambiguity (55). He ends this description by concluding that in all reality, Court Street "was the only Brooklyn, really—north was Brooklyn Heights, secretly a part of Manhattan" (56). James Peacock argues that Lionel's setting of boundaries on the "real" Brooklyn constitutes "a kind of gerrymandering" that Lionel uses strategically with the goal of preserving "preconceived notions of what constitutes the essential, authentic Brooklyn."[15] While this is true to a point, I would add that this happens largely because Lionel equates Court Street with Minna and vice versa, and he credits both with bringing him out of the St. Vincent's library and into the world. As he becomes a Minna Man, the two (that is, the man and the street, together) "had begun to draw me out" (57). The "real" Brooklyn may be defined in tautological terms—it is real because I say it is real—but Lionel defines it in this way because he attributes so much of his ability to function as an adult to Minna and his guidance.

Lionel takes his cues from Minna, which is to say from Court Street and from Brooklyn. Lionel even borrows personal preferences from Minna, for whom "the Yankees were holy but boring, the Mets wonderfully pathetic and human" (*MB* 67). The comparison here is not Brooklyn to Manhattan but the scrappy lovable losers to the wealthy institution, indicating Minna's (and, by clear extension, Lionel's) more general alignment with underdogs. Tony will later tell Lionel in accusation, "Everything you know comes from Frank Minna or a book," and Lionel does not take it entirely as an insult (184). Even later, after calling Minna "the secret king of Court Street," Lionel will make his identification complete, with intentional echoes of Flaubert: "*Frank Minna c'est moi*" (214). As much as Lethem has revealed himself in *Motherless Brooklyn* to be under the distinct influence of Raymond Chandler, and as Lethem tells us that Minna read Chandler too, Lethem reveals Lionel in turn to be under the same readerly spell Even if he takes that influence secondhand through Minna, Lionel's identification with Minna is so complete that the secondhand influence becomes a direct one.

I have deliberately avoided revealing too much here about the detailed mechanics of this novel's murder plot. For purposes of explaining, as this chapter aims to do, how Lethem is riffing on Chandler while developing these career-long interests in the cultural space of New York City and how people incorporate the art that influences them into their lives, suffice it to say that the disparate clues and details Lionel uncovers in his investigation do get fully explained near the novel's end. Not coincidentally, Lethem sends Lionel well outside of New York City in order to uncover this information fully, and also not coincidentally, Lethem momentarily suspends Lionel's narration, lapsing into a third-person point of view for six pages in order to provide some much-desired exposition about Frank and Gerard Minna's early lives. When we return to Lionel's point of view, it becomes clear that Frank's widow Julia has told Lionel this story offstage, so to speak. Readers have been waiting for this big reveal for quite a while, as the occasional recaps of what Lionel has figured out—an old detective novelist's trick for helping a reader keep track of what has been learned and what is left to discover—tend to frustrate. Not long after Minna's death, Lionel reviews the notes he has taken in his notebook and realizes that as clues they are "paperthin and unrevealing" (*MB* 95). Later he will mull over a set of "paltry clues" (118), and one of few remaining attempts to recap this intricate plot consists solely of questions (246), implying that Lionel has discovered little of value at all.

In true Chandleresque mystery novel fashion, these pieces begin to fall clearly into place mostly in a single paragraph (*MB* 289). Per Chandler's "Twelve Notes on the Mystery Story," a mystery's hidden plot machinery "must have enough essential simplicity to be explained easily when the time comes. . . . The ideal denouement is one in which everything is revealed in a flash of action." The explanation "must be interesting in itself, it must be something the reader is anxious to hear, and not a new story with a new set of characters, dragged in to justify an overcomplicated plot. Above all the explanation must not be merely a long-winded assembling of minute circumstances which no ordinary reader could possibly be expected to remember."[16] Here, Lethem returns to the classic hard-boiled playbook, with Lionel learning all he needs to know from the character he describes fatalistically as "the hardest-boiled of us all" and "maybe the unhappiest person I'd ever met" (303).

There is left for Lionel, though, the matter of how to take in this new information, which he sees as altering considerably how he understands his own past, particularly Minna's kindness to him as a young man. Peacock reads Lionel's next actions as a rejection of the past he now understands better. Lionel, he argues, "flings the detritus of the case—his and Julia's guns, his cell phone, Minna's pager—into the ocean in a symbolic act of catharsis and consignment of the past to the past (albeit one partly driven by physical compulsion)."[17] Physical compulsion indeed: in a wry seriocomic coda to this jettisoning of the past, Lionel, who has spent the whole novel obsessively needing to do things in groups of five, needs one more thing to throw into the sea, so he chooses one of his shoes, leaving him lacking one shoe all the way back to Brooklyn. For Lethem's reflective male protagonists, figuring out one's attitude toward a complicated personal past is akin to (and sometimes directly involves) figuring out what to do with artistic influence. In Lionel's case, this sudden introspection forces him to articulate his relationships to Minna and, by extension, to Chandler. Peacock continues, "Seen in this way, detective fiction in *Motherless Brooklyn* succumbs to the same temptation as it does in *Gun, with Occasional Music:* to attribute such importance to the past, to remembering, that a sense of historical evolution is sacrificed to a contrived sense of timelessness."[18] Here I disagree with Peacock, who appears to be seeing in Lethem's work more pious reverence for genre fiction's roots and history than I find visible there.

Lethem knows his Chandler and Hammett, as he reminds us frequently in interviews and nonfiction. But by no means does *Motherless Brooklyn* become a period piece or a by-the-numbers exercise in hip retro writing either. First of all, textual details such as Lionel's cell phone and CD player place this novel firmly in or near the period of its publication, the 1990s. If there is nostalgia here, Lethem has not succumbed to the easiest nostalgic mode possible, one that invokes the past by invoking readers' stereotypes about the past. In fact Lionel in his obsessiveness is particularly attuned to anachronisms around him. He recalls initial meetings with Frank Minna as a teenager in which he noted Minna's "smooth pompadour," which "stood completely outside that year of 1979" (*MB* 40). Lionel respects Minna, but he registers that hairstyle as unusual, no doubt. Second, the attachment to the past that is visible here is selective and thoughtful: Lionel gladly tosses Minna's pager into the ocean but decides that he must keep Minna's watch, to which he confesses a sentimental attachment (303).

Most of all, though, this is a novel that understands and articulates clearly its own relationship to detective fiction of the past. We know, from the backstory about Minna and his brother revealed in the mystery's denouement, that Frank was a reader of hard-boiled novels, "Spillane and Chandler and Ross MacDonald" (*MB* 288). If Frank gained from reading those books any real knowledge about how the world works, however, this did not help him avoid involvement in a complex, somewhat conspiratorial plot that results in his murder. Lionel, though, not only makes it to the end of the novel alive but also thrives, functioning in the last pages as part of a working surrogate family. The pairing of Minna's death with Lionel's survival suggests that real danger exists in playing one's cards too slavishly by the noir playbook. Put another way, Minna, more the stereotypical small-time hood of noir fiction than Lionel is the stereotypical noir hero, gets killed off; Lionel, who looks just like a hard-boiled detective in certain ways and not at all like one in others, suffers loss but comes to terms with it.

The idea that Lionel leaves his past fully behind in Maine as he hears how the pieces of the novel's mystery fit together is contradicted by the novel's final pages. After fully investigating Minna's death, Lionel returns to Court Street, Brooklyn, happy to report that he, Gilbert, and Danny now run "a detective agency, a clean one for the first time" (*MB* 306). Lionel has left behind Minna's shady connections and illegal deals, but he has found an identity as a detective that he is proud to hang on to. It is important to note, however, that the ending has its ominous details. Yes, Lionel does explain to us that he is now part of a real agency, run by the surviving Minna Men and not a front for any illegal business. The dominant scene in the novel's last chapter depicts Lionel and his associates playing poker in the wee hours of the morning. As Lionel tries to win a hand holding two pairs—jacks and twos—Gilbert counters with aces and eights, joshing to Lionel, "Read 'em and scream, like the maniac you are" (*MB* 307). The balance of this largely positive ending is disrupted, however, by Gilbert's winning cards: aces and eights, after all, are the "dead man's hand," allegedly held by Wild Bill Hickok when he was murdered in Old West legend. Like so many details in Lethem's fiction—and particularly like so many details in *The Fortress of Solitude,* the novel I will focus on next—Gilbert's cards may read at first like a throwaway bit of incidental business. However, they bear a highly specific meaning to readers in the know, particularly readers well versed in particular kinds of masculine, pop-centric lore.

CHAPTER 3

The Fortress of Solitude

Experience and Interpretation

In reviewing Lethem's *The Fortress of Solitude* (2003) for the September 21, 2003, edition of the *New York Times,* the critic A. O. Scott remarked that *Motherless Brooklyn* might be a more appropriate title for the newer book than was the comic book reference for which Lethem opted (the actual title refers to Superman's secret lair and sometimes headquarters). I am inclined to agree: even more so than *Motherless Brooklyn, The Fortress of Solitude* is about surrogate families and the complexity of understanding the cultural space of New York City. *The Fortress of Solitude* incorporates a wide variety of Lethem's influences more overtly and more complexly than its predecessors, however; it highlights Lethem's career-long interests in the racial politics of popular culture as well as the joys and dangers of passionate consumption and intellectual appreciation of cultural artifacts. It is also a book in which every imaginable personal choice—where to live, where to attend school, whom to consider a friend, how to dress, and what culture to consume, especially what music to listen to—has inescapable political baggage. This is a book, after all, with a main character who was once in a singing group called the Subtle Distinctions.[1] In *The Fortress of Solitude* the personal is political and then some.

Because *The Fortress of Solitude* evokes with such detail urban childhoods, the gritty and embattled New York of the 1970s, and the utopian idealisms of any number of attempted utopias, many reviewers thought of the novel upon its publication as Lethem's turn from the sci-fi margins of the literary landscape to a more naturalistic mainstream. For example, in an otherwise ambivalent-to-negative *New York Review of Books* piece with the crankily dismissive title "Welcome to New Dork," John Leonard compares Lethem's early sci-fi to *The Fortress of Solitude*'s brownstones and aspiring artists and concludes that Lethem has "shape-changed from Kurt Vonnegut into Saul Bellow before our starry eyes."[2] To assert that, though, is to buy into a false dichotomy between the fantastic and the realistic that hardly holds true in Lethem's work, given that even his most eccentric fictions have quite grounded elements, while his most grounded ones still have their oddities. Lethem admirably resists this artificial distinction: he has commented that while he is well aware that many people read *Motherless Brooklyn* as a basically realist text, "it's quite absurd to believe that these guys are lurking around Brooklyn in trench coats acting like detectives, or that there are Zen Buddhist Mafiosi" (*Conv* 110). Similarly he ended a 2001 interview by saying of the work in progress that would become *The Fortress of Solitude,* "I'm headed toward a fantastic which is grained like realism, which everywhere makes feints of realism" (44–45). Eventually he concluded, "So I'm becoming a realist. Right? Right. I said it. There. Except there are going to be superheroes" (45). Simply put, readers ought to be careful not to draw two broad columns marked "realism" and "fantasy" respectively and then promptly place *The Fortress of Solitude* in the realist category. After all, this allegedly realist novel has a magic ring that grants the powers of flight and invisibility.

At plot level, *The Fortress of Solitude* is far easier to summarize than *Motherless Brooklyn* is. The novel's first of three parts describes the childhood, from roughly age five to age eighteen, of Dylan Ebdus, who grows up in the rapidly gentrifying Boerum Hill neighborhood of Brooklyn in the 1970s. His father Abraham is emotionally absent, constantly working on a hand-painted experimental film and later taking up painting garish covers for sci-fi novels to pay the bills. His mother Rachel is physically absent, having run away with the nephew of the neighborhood's developer early in the novel, even though the family has settled in Brooklyn and enrolled Dylan in the New York public schools at Rachel's well-meaningly liberal, if naive, insistence. In this ethnically diverse neighborhood, the quasi-bohemian Ebduses are in the minority as a white family. Dylan's disorienting experience of feeling like an outsider nearly everywhere he goes will color his upbringing and eventually his entire life.

Dylan's closest friend in Boerum Hill is Mingus Rude, the son of Barrett Rude Jr., an aging soul singer who moves to Brooklyn with Mingus following a costly divorce. Barrett's fundamentalist preacher father later joins them in Brooklyn, creating family conflict since Barrett Sr. has little patience with his son's casual drug use and promiscuity. Dylan and Mingus become fast friends, bonding over a shared love of then-current soul music of the 1970s, the burgeoning renegade art form of New York graffiti tagging, and crucially, if not most importantly to Dylan and Mingus, comic books. After a chance encounter with a homeless man (who might be a failed superhero himself), the two boys are given a magical ring, which they discover grants its wearer the powers of flight and, later, invisibility. The shared secret of the ring helps bond this cross-racial friendship, even as Dylan and Mingus grow apart. Meanwhile, Dylan's only close white friend, Arthur Lomb, gradually becomes less and less a stereotypical white nerd and more and more a "Mingus-puppet" *(TFoS* 190), adopting elements of African American style, spending ever more time with Mingus than with Dylan, and eventually embracing Mingus's passions for graffiti and cocaine.

The novel's brief second part appears in the guise of the liner notes to a reissue of Barrett Rude Jr.'s greatest hits, written by the adult Dylan Ebdus, who has grown up to become a music journalist and wannabe screenwriter. Lethem uses this unusual form to illuminate a key plot point left unrevealed by the third part's closing cliff-hanger. Part 3 leaves behind part 1's first-person narration as Dylan starts telling his own story. He recounts his one semester at (and subsequent expulsion from) the fictional Camden College and his visits back to Brooklyn and to a sci-fi convention at which his father is honored. He ultimately decides to use the ring's power in an attempt to set free the now-incarcerated Mingus Rude. The first-person narration is briefly replaced with third-person narration as Lethem fills in the gaps in our knowledge about the life led by Mingus after Dylan left Brooklyn behind. Significantly, Mingus is referred to in those sections only as "Dose," Mingus's old graffiti tag.

More than any other Lethem novel to this point, *The Fortress of Solitude* is rooted in the specifics of a physical setting and its inhabitants, drawn with great precision. The sheer amount of detail can be overwhelming, as can the overflowing energy with which Lethem describes details of 1970s Brooklyn, but all of this information about place is necessary, both for establishing location and for clarifying Lethem's attitude toward this place. Evan Hughes contrasts the joy of Lethem's *The Fortress of Solitude,* however, against two other major novels about gentrifying Brooklyn in the 1970s that were both set and published in that decade. L. J. Davis's *A Meaningful Life* (1971), a book for which Lethem wrote an introduction, reprinted in *The Ecstasy of Influence,* on its reissue by the New York Review Books imprint, and Paula Fox's *Desperate Characters* (1970) are both worthwhile reads for anyone interested in a nervier, pricklier, less nostalgic take on the class and racial politics of gentrification. For Hughes, Lethem displays "a reverie and nostalgia"; largely because of the youthful worldview of the novel's protagonist in part 1, Lethem's "writing is jazzy, loose, even exuberant."[3] Dylan as an adult—that is to say, as a music writer by profession, a professional appreciator, and an influence hound—cannot be fully understood without first understanding the formative experiences of his youth, all of which are bound up in his social circles and location.

New York is symbolic cultural space in *The Fortress of Solitude,* as it was in *Motherless Brooklyn,* but even more so it is a site of visible, depicted lived realities of race, class, and most of all gentrification. "Underberg," the title of part 1 of *The Fortress of Solitude,* refers literally to a grocery supply store in Flatbush where young taggers can buy a particular kind of industrial-strength ink for use in makeshift graffiti markers (*TFoS* 186). More metaphorically, it reminds readers that compared to Manhattan, a borough far more synonymous with "New York City" in the minds of many, Dylan's Brooklyn is a kind of "under-city," perhaps less prominent but every bit as full of vibrant and multifaceted life. That said, Brooklyn is a place in flux from the novel's first pages. Before readers meet Dylan's parents even, Lethem introduces Isabel Vendle, an "old white woman" who has moved to the Ebduses' neighborhood "to reclaim one of the abused buildings" (3) and who serves as the novel's face of thoughtless gentrification; she fears minorities and judges the success of the neighborhood's transformation by the number of white faces she sees. To her apparent delight, "white people were returning to Dean Street. A few" (4). She begins a campaign to rebrand the neighborhood, wanting to replace the name Gowanus with Boerum Hill wherever possible: "Isabel Vendle found the name in a tattered, leather-bound volume at the Brooklyn Historical Society: Boerum. As in the Boer War," she thinks, evidently blind to the colonialist bent of the comparison (7).

Vendle's attitude toward gentrification requires thinking of the health of a neighborhood solely in physical, even infrastructural terms. She values the physicality of the neighborhood's buildings over any people in them. "The houses here were sick," she thinks, and later she describes a workman restoring a ceiling as "an instrument of the ceiling. He doesn't need to understand" (*TFoS* 7, 18). Her distaste for Dean Street as it currently exists is bodily and visceral: "she wished she could paste money over the blue siding which stung her eyes like ointment" (25). The corporeal metaphors continue as she claims that "her body was Boerum Hill, just as King Arthur's body had been England" (61). Three pages later she is dead, failing to live to see Gowanus become Boerum Hill as she desired.

Isabel's striving conservatism stands in contrast to the grounded, if naive, liberalism of Dylan's mother Rachel. "Rachel had a program, a plan," we are told. "She had grown up a Brooklyn street kid and so would Dylan" (*TFoS* 12–13). Her interest in Dylan having an upbringing comparable to her own is intense yet sincere. Even as not everyone in Brooklyn understands her motives—her friends include a "woman from the Brooklyn Heights consciousness-raising group who just couldn't believe they'd bought on Dean Street" (12)—Rachel wants Dylan to understand (though perhaps at too early an age) the complexities of the contours of his neighborhood and her politics. The novel's first use of the word "gentrification" occurs as Rachel teaches Dylan to disdain the term. Our narrator notes, "This was a Nixon word, uncool," while Rachel's disdain for Vendle's pet project is even stronger: "Boerum Hill is pretentious bullshit" (52). After attempting to inculcate in Dylan this liberalism, grounded in an unequivocally positive view of Dean Street as a place for a great childhood, Rachel leaves Abraham for whereabouts yet unknown, though she begins sending Dylan cryptic postcards signed "Running Crab." Without her, Brooklyn remains the same in some ways, as in a wonderful description of a dilapidated theater that is a "grand ruin of an Art Deco movie palace" now showing blaxploitation flicks (109). In other moments gentrification accelerates big changes in the neighborhood, culminating in *New York Magazine* calling Boerum Hill "The City's Best-Kept Secret" (135). Early in the novel, at least, arguments about gentrification are the sole province of Isabel and Rachel. In his excellent explanation of how gentrification works in *The Fortress of Solitude,* Matt Godbey makes a strong case that "Lethem positions Dylan's story—his history with and alienation from Gowanus/Boerum Hill—as the story of the neighborhood's gentrification," when the stories of Dean Street's nonwhite residents are equally valid and equally important to understanding this process.[4] It is true that Lethem depicts Mingus working for a short time helping restore Brooklyn houses, ironically making him complicit in the ethically questionable act of gentrification. Even this episode, though, serves as a foil to Dylan's experiences elsewhere, Dylan having left Brooklyn by then.

Events in part 3 of the novel will reveal to Dylan the problems with his tendency, enamored as he is with soul music and what he imagines as "authentic" Brooklyn, to fetishize blackness. Those seeds were of course planted by Rachel, who "was working the block, matchmaking for him" in the novel's opening pages, seemingly making a point of finding Dylan some nonwhite friends in the neighborhood in response to Dylan's interest in the two young blond girls on the block (*TFoS* 5). Rachel will insist on public school for Dylan and boast with awed pride that Dylan is "one of three white children in the whole school. . . . Not his class, not his grade—the whole school" (18, 24). When the Rude family moves to the street, Isabel describes Barrett as "that beautiful black man who moved in next to Isabel Vendle" and instantly proclaims that Barrett's son Mingus is "going to be your new best friend, that's my prediction" (54). This attitude of Isabel's has its limits, which are displayed when she smacks around a bit Robert Woolfolk, a black kid from the area who will become a frequent presence in Dylan's life, for stealing Dylan's bicycle (46), an incident that becomes instant neighborhood legend.

Dylan's childhood is inescapably racialized in nearly every regard, as Dylan becomes ever more hyperaware of how unusual his situation is: as one of few white kids on Dean Street, Dylan grasps the irony of being in a statistical majority in a broad sense while also feeling like a minority in a more local sense. Among Dylan's earliest memories is seeing those two blond neighbors and "wonder[ing] guiltily why the white girls on skates hadn't called to him instead" of the African American kids who become his closer friends; early in chapter 2, though, those white girls have moved away anyway *(TFoS* 6). Lethem narrates ruefully, "So at the very start the circle shrank" (23).

In introducing Dylan's point of view early in the chapter of *Literary Brooklyn* (2011) about Brooklyn of the 1970s, Evan Hughes notes, "Malcolm X, Dr. King, and Bobby Kennedy have all been shot dead, and anyway they're just names to these young kids. They're more familiar with the attitudes and ground-level realities the civil rights era didn't fix."[5] In other words, Dylan, Mingus, Arthur, and Robert alike lack the vocabulary as kids to recognize the roots or history of urban racism, but they know it when they see it. Hughes points out that major race riots occurred in Newark, Detroit, Chicago, and Washington, D.C., in the late 1960s. Add New York City's well-documented financial troubles, most famously culminating in President Gerald Ford's refusal to bail out the city and the iconic *New York Daily News* headline "Ford to City: Drop Dead," to the list of the city's urban woes, and New York in the 1970s becomes a place of considerable (if sometimes sublimated) racial tension.[6] Hughes points out that Brooklyn had been "stricken by economic stagnation and [was] home to more black residents than any other borough," likening parts of Brooklyn to "dry tinder ready for a spark."[7] While *The Fortress of Solitude* is not a text in which racial tension ever ignites to a full-grown blaze, Dylan remains constantly aware of how fraught cross-racial interaction can be. To claim friendship with Mingus can come across (as it sometimes does) as using him; to deny his intimacy with Mingus can come across as xenophobic.

That double bind is at the center of one of the novel's recurring incidents and guiding metaphors: yoking. Lethem simultaneously introduces yoking as basically innocent schoolboy high jinks, on the one hand, and as a near-daily forced entry into a minefield of racialized behavior, on the other hand. Comparable to a low-stakes mugging, the guiding principle of yoking is that it is highly scripted, with actor and victim taking predetermined roles. An acquaintance of Dylan's, generally an African American one, puts him in a playful headlock or verbally accosts him and then asks for a dollar or some small possession. If Dylan refuses to cooperate, the yoker has a convenient out: he can accusingly ask Dylan what he is afraid of or, more to the point, double down on that question by making it less playful and more accusatory: "What you afraid of? You a *racist,* man?" (*TFoS* 85). Dylan cannot win either way. He is either separated from his pocket change, having willfully and pathetically succumbed to victimhood, or if he resists, he passively subjugates the yoker through the innuendo of racism. This suggestion that cross-racial interaction is doomed to be a no-win game for Dylan (or at best, an always politically touchy proposition) recurs throughout his life. If he rejects the polycultural world that he has grown up with and around on Dean Street, that act can easily be interpreted as racist. If he embraces it all too readily, then he can veer into the trap of cultural appropriation that is more quasi-colonialist than creative. The adult Dylan sees this in his African American girlfriend's accusation, early in part 3, that he embraces her more for the cultural symbol of her blackness than for her as a person or a partner. When Dylan pitches a screenplay idea to a Hollywood studio exec, a musical biopic about the Prisonaires, a real 1950s doo-wop group who also happened to be incarcerated, this political question bubbles up to the surface again. Is Dylan shining a light on a fascinating but lesser-known slice of African American history, or is he using it only to make a name for himself?

While these difficulties of cultural appropriation are important to Lethem, particularly since they constitute one way of approaching the question of what one is to do with one's influences, it is not advisable to focus on race in *The Fortress of Solitude* to the exclusion of class. After all, as explosive as the issue of gentrification is for those interested in racial inequalities, its effects are perhaps even more visible in its exacerbation of economic inequalities. Dylan's first inklings of recognition that class differences exist are rather typical for his age. He wants "Pro Ked 69ers" as "satisfying badges of legitimacy," as opposed to any cheap no-name sneakers (*TFoS* 89). He soon starts noticing prep school kids in Brooklyn Heights with their "Lacoste shirts and corduroys, suede jacket sleeves knotted at their waists," ever the brand-conscious adolescent (91). By the time he is ready for college, though, he has chosen Camden College, based on Vermont's Bennington College, which Lethem attended for less than two years. Lethem's Bennington classmate Bret Easton Ellis originated the depiction of a thinly veiled Bennington as Camden in *Less than Zero* and developed it further in his second novel, *The Rules of Attraction;* Jill Eisenstadt too has made use of the setting, in *From Rockaway.* Lethem's Camden, the adult Dylan narrates, is "one part experimental arts college" and "one part lunatic preserve for wayward children of privilege" (383). The teenaged Dylan wants in for the same reasons: its "weird disreputability and allure of pure dollars" (272). He also now openly covets upward mobility. "If a kid from Gowanus goes to the most expensive college in America," he thinks, "maybe he's from Boerum Hill after all" (272). Once there, however, he realizes that he is "class-dumb, protected from any understanding of money by my father's artisan-elitism and, paradoxically, by Rachel's radical populist pride" (383). As a defense mechanism, he performs that lack of knowledge about wealth to the hilt, pretending to have never heard of resort towns and not to recognize the names of wealthy families (389). He pushes his wealthy classmates even further by openly discussing their privilege in their presence, realizing that he displays an aggression in doing so that leaves them "flattered and appalled" in equal measure (390). Lethem reminds us that much subtler items serve as class markers as well. Much later, when he goes to visit Mingus in jail, Dylan has to empty his pockets for security reasons. A guard does not recognize the odd foam-rubber trinket Dylan has just produced, and as Dylan stammers to explain his desire to sleep on his cross-country flight, what dawns on him is "the bourgeois implications of an earplug" (442).

These class barriers remain visible throughout *The Fortress of Solitude* even as Dylan finds ways to transcend them in searching for surrogate families to replace his broken family at home. Surrogate families in Lethem, such as the Minna Men of *Motherless Brooklyn,* tend to be loving but dysfunctional, necessary but frustrating. Above all they tend to be communities of like-minded outcasts. After passing a challenging aptitude test to gain entry into a selective Manhattan public school, Dylan finds at Stuyvesant a brainy surrogate family that is simultaneously diverse in ethnicity but homogeneous in its intellectual power: his new school "was Jewish white, Wasp white, hippie white, Chinese, black, Puerto Rican, and much else but crucially it was nerd, nerd, nerd, nerd, the great family of those able to ace the entrance test" *(TFoS* 220). Also important for Dylan's upbringing is how instantly Stuyvesant increases his sense of access to a broader world, as the school "drew high-scorers from all five boroughs" (219). His growing familiarity with Manhattan puts him in contact with aesthetic experiences that act as influences on him for the rest of his life: he goes to midnight movies at repertory houses and passes rock clubs while wondering what other worlds they represent (221).

In part 3 Dylan finds another surrogate family at the Berkeley college radio station where he works. The cohort of disc jockeys there have "the depth of an anarchic family" (*TFoS* 406), but this anarchic family is awkwardly social, "a hermetic community at best" (409). Like most small subcultures in *The Fortress of Solitude,* including comic book readers and sci-fi junkies, these college-radio rock geeks are insular and even a bit aggressive in their insistence on the primacy of their taste. After all, it takes considerable certainty in one's own artistic preferences to make one build a broadcasted program around them. In addition surrogate families are quite significantly not limited only to Dylan's experience. In part 3 Lethem depicts the imprisoned Mingus being reunited, with some warmth and familiarity, with other New York graffiti writers whom he had known (if not in person, then by their tags) in his youth (485).

The novel's most important nonfamily relationship remains Dylan's alternately warm and troubled friendship with Mingus. Read most idyllically, Dylan and Mingus became a late entry in the long American literary tradition of idealized cross-racial friendship. We can add them to the list that begins with Natty Bumppo and Chingachgook in the works of James Fenimore Cooper, Ishmael and Queequeg in Herman Melville, and Huck and Jim in Mark Twain; or perhaps more appropriately, as Lethem invokes comic book archetypes, the cross-racial duos of "Captain America and Falcon, Iron Fist and Luke Cage" (*TFoS* 79). And like those central friendships in Melville and Twain particularly, Mingus and Dylan's relationship occasionally crosses over from the homosocial to the homoerotic. They engage in some adolescent sexual experimentation, on one occasion awkwardly interrupted by Barrett (209, 225). Much later, seeing Mingus in prison as an adult, Dylan recalls Mingus as "the rejected idol of my entire youth, my best friend, my lover" (443). Dylan and Mingus take their places in this long tradition of intensely passionate cross-racial friendships only if they are interpreted as a dynamic duo, a unified whole.

Lethem encourages readers, however, to approach this interpretation carefully, as he depicts Dylan and Mingus even more frequently in ways that emphasize irreconcilable differences between the pair. The racialized cultural space of 1970s Brooklyn, he reminds us, enables Dylan and Mingus to maintain consistent and even occasionally intimate contact, but in no way are the two boys promised equal opportunity. By the time they both enter their respective high schools, "Sarah J. Hale" and "Stuyvesant" serve as synecdoches for how divergent their futures are already shaping up to be: Mingus attends a failing high school, one compared to prison by the young, preminstrelized Arthur Lomb (*TFoS* 126), foreshadowing where Mingus will end up literally; meanwhile Dylan hops boroughs daily to Stuyvesant, where his life in Brooklyn seems "untellable" to his classmates (229). Around this time Dylan notices that Mingus might "vanish for weeks, then [they]'d meet up" and spend a whole day together, not having missed a step (198), testament both to the durability of their bond and to their growing ever further apart. For Evan Hughes, these stresses on their friendship reveal that the "divisions that Dylan's parents and so many sixties progressives hoped to overcome" still bear great power.[8] Indeed, Dylan comes to realize in adulthood how misguided his parents' idealism (and by logical extension then, hippie utopianism more generally) wound up being, calling utopia "the show which always closed on opening night" (510). In following these diverging paths all the way to the novel's end, James Peacock suggests a more deterministic view: that since Dylan winds up a working music writer while Mingus is incarcerated, such contrasts "only serve to exacerbate the racial delineations in operation."[9] I disagree, given that the boundary lines separating races in *The Fortress of Solitude* are considerably more permeable than such a reading would imply.

Indeed one of the more curiously underdiscussed aspects of *The Fortress of Solitude* is that Lethem provides considerable evidence that Mingus is multiracial. Mingus confirms in his first appearance in the novel that he was the subject of the custody battle at the middle of Barrett's messy divorce: "That's what he had to pay to get me back, a million cold" (*TFoS* 57). "Liner Note" fills in some key details: Barrett met Junie Kwarsh, his wife and the subject (or as it were, object) of Barrett's postdivorce record *Take It, Baby,* during an early stint as a Memphis disc jockey. Junie was "the daughter of the station's white owner" (297). Given this information, which Lethem does force the reader to piece together gradually, Mingus becomes much more difficult to pigeonhole into a binary understanding of race. As a result, deterministic readings of the novel's racial politics, which see Mingus's fall into addiction and incarceration as every bit as inevitable as Dylan's relative success, become harder to support.

Additionally, Arthur Lomb functions as an intermediary between these two extremes; even more the white nerd than Dylan when they first meet, he winds up performing an ersatz assumed African American identity more artificially than Dylan ever does. His chameleonlike nature, though, not his whiteness, is what lets him go to Sarah J. Hale with Mingus without succumbing to the same temptations as does Mingus (who, after all, never had to look further than his father for access to drugs). When Dylan meets Arthur, the fairly successful owner of a small Brooklyn restaurant in the novel's present, Dylan notices Arthur's Yankees cap and reflects, "I still hadn't forgiven him his flip-flop from Mets fandom when we were twelve. That betrayal stood, in my mind, for Arthur's easy adaptation to black style, his glomming onto Mingus Rude. The same inhibition that stuck me to the losing Mets had barred me from the minstrelsy which would have allowed me to follow Mingus where he was going" (*TFoS* 431). In other words, Dylan realizes that had he so fully identified with Mingus and all that Mingus loved (including not only funk music and graffiti but also cocaine), he may well be in jail too. Ironically, though, Arthur, not Mingus, comes out of this reverie having "betray[ed]" Dean Street, despite having stayed in Brooklyn, still involved in the borough's ongoing rebirth. For all of Dylan's frustration with Mingus, Dylan at least finds Mingus to have been more consistent than Arthur. We know Dylan to be frustrated by inconsistency in his friends: he "never met anyone who wasn't about to change immediately into someone else" (232). When Dylan sees Mingus in jail, though, he sees his childhood friend. When he sees Arthur in his restaurant, he does not see the kid who once beat him at chess.

As fraught as this central friendship can be, certain aspects of Dylan's relationship with Mingus contain little visible racial baggage. In Hughes's reading, Mingus "puts Dylan in reach of the social life he craves among the cool kids who look nothing like him. Mingus gives him cover in the neighborhood when he wants to join the crowd."[10] What is remarkable about this statement is how true it is while also removing racial difference from the picture altogether. The core of the relationship (that is, less cool kid knows he is less cool, seeks entry into the cool clique through the help of a generous cooler friend) is familiar to anyone who can recognize how schoolyard friendships—*any* schoolyard's friendships—work. It does appear that Mingus and Dylan's friendship works just that way at first, particularly in their earliest interactions, in which Dylan functions briefly as the more streetwise kid. Mingus appears to Dylan initially as a quintessential suburban kid who will need, ironically enough, Dylan's protection on Dean Street. Mingus shows Dylan his team uniforms from youth sports leagues, recalling organized sports that contrast wildly against the looser and less structured street games Dylan has grown up playing. Mingus seems a nice kid, "but can you catch a spaldeen?" Dylan wonders (*TFoS* 55). Dylan is unimpressed with those uniforms, because Mingus plays the wrong games: baseball and football instead of stoopball and stickball.

Ultimately what most effectively and definitively binds Dylan and Mingus as friends is the ownership of a magical ring that grants the wearer the ability to fly. Some readers see this unmistakable stroke of the fantastic, borrowing clearly from the tropes of superhero comics, as an unnecessary intrusion of sci-fi into an otherwise largely realist novel. Others, myself included, understand it as having narrative functions that become so central to the book that it cannot be dismissed as marginal. Lethem first associates comic fandom not in Dylan or Mingus but in Rachel, who briefly shares her enthusiasm with Isabel Vendle's nephew Croft (*TFoS* 39–40). Later, Rachel's confrontation with Robert Woolfolk is narrated from a bird's-eye view, "the perspective of a flying man" (46). Gradually, Lethem starts locating comic fandom more often in Dylan, particularly as he reports seeing multiple times a "ragged figure arching from the roof of Public School 38. . . . He looked like a bum" (54). The origin story in which Dylan and Mingus gain their unlikely superpower is signaled as "the day the flying man falls from the roof" (101). Meanwhile, Lethem occasionally refers to Dylan as "Mole-boy" in the lead-up to the origin story. Literally, he is describing Dylan's appearance when he is bundled up in a parka against the cold. Figuratively, the name suggests a latent superhero identity, contrasting with the mild-mannered alter ego Dylan Ebdus. Indeed a homeless man falls out of the sky that day, and Dylan notices the ring on his finger (101). Later, Abraham will notice Mingus's graffiti tag on the man's sleeping bag and take offense to the idea that he and Dylan have tagged a person, showing such "disrespect for a human life" (143). Abraham takes him to a doctor, where we learn that the man's name is Aaron X. Doily and where he surrenders the ring to Dylan, saying, "I'm done, I'm *through,* man. Cain't fight the *air waves*" (149). Dylan is fairly certain that Doily admonishes him to "*Fight evil!*" (150).

Dylan and Mingus create a superhero together, christened Aeroman, complete with homemade supersuit. They make use of the ring somewhat regularly, though Mingus tends to be the more adept flyer. Dylan wears the ring for one memorably dominant performance in a stoopball game, briefly echoing back to "Vanilla Dunk," and later flies alone during a summer in Vermont (*TFoS* 162). Mingus uses the ring more frequently in part 1, and he indeed attempts to fight crime. "Aeroman flew six or seven times that fall, was perhaps involved in eight or nine incidents, could claim maybe three bona fide rescues, legible crimes authentically flown down on and busted up," Lethem reports (225). Along the way, Mingus learns that the ring grants him the ability to swim also, and after he unknowingly breaks up a drug deal that was actually an undercover police sting operation, Mingus as Aeroman makes the *New York Times* (236). He also manages to produce a three-story-tall graffiti tag over ten stories above the ground on the side of the Brooklyn House of Detention (274). Upon hearing that Robert Woolfolk tried the ring once but flew poorly, Dylan realizes, "The ring was not a neutral tool. It judged its wearer: Aaron Doily flew drunkenly, and Dylan flew like a coward, only when it didn't matter" (285–86). As an adult in part 3, Dylan discovers that the ring's power has switched from flight to invisibility. With this knowledge and new superpower, he makes a quixotic attempt to stem the crack epidemic of the 1980s and gets involved in the shooting of a dealer, earning in the news the unknown "urban avenger" comparisons to the New York subway vigilante Bernhard Goetz (420, 421). To its users the ring grants power that is real but often uncontrollable.

Lethem's use of comics in this novel has generated perhaps more critical attention than any other single element of the text. For David Coughlan, changes in characters' attitudes toward comics mirror their growing awareness of racial difference. Early in the novel, he argues, comics have imaginative value in that they "offer a world without a discriminating gender or racial bias."[11] By the end of part 1, as Dylan buys Mingus's comic collection, spending some of his college savings to help finance Mingus and Arthur's drug deal, they bear monetary use value primarily, as these characters now "more closely correspond to types predicated on forms of rigid social categorisation based on race and class."[12] Marc Singer's reading is less congratulatory, asserting that Lethem's invocations of superhero comics are "far less sophisticated in their modes of signification and their narrative structure than the comics they purport to represent."[13] But that is because the thing Singer values in superhero comics is their visual images' ability to represent reality without having to resort to unstable, metaphorical language. Lethem has suggested that ultimately all language is unavoidably metaphorical anyway: "Fiction, like language, is innately artificial and innately fabulous. It's made of metaphor" (*Conv* 128). Lethem would likely respond that no written fiction could do what the comic book can, so a reader who expects an innovative literary novel to bear the same kind of sophistication as an innovative graphic novel will always wind up being disappointed.

The entire concept of Aeroman would not have come into the minds of Dylan and Mingus, even owning Aaron Doily's ring, unless they had already been conversant in the tropes of superhero comics. Dylan and Mingus bond over comic books on their first meeting, helping lead Dylan to compare elements of his own life to that of a superhero: "Superman in his Fortress of Solitude reminded [him] all too much of Abraham in his high studio," Lethem narrates, in the first of only two uses of the title phrase in the novel (*TFoS* 55, 66). Comic books function in *The Fortress of Solitude* as a literal detail at the center of young friendships, as a source of narrative archetypes, and as an art form that provides inspiration and influence to the novel's artist figures, particularly Mingus, the aspiring graffiti writer.

Lethem introduces Mingus's newly found passion for graffiti rather matter-of-factly. Dylan notices one day that Mingus's possessions are now covered in "ballpoint scrawlings," and Mingus calmly responds, "It's my tag, Dose. It's what I write" (*TFoS* 72). Soon Dylan starts tagging too, but significantly, he does not create a tag of his own, opting instead to mimic Mingus's tag, Dose. It is the first major example in the novel of Dylan appropriating African American style and using it to create for himself a new identity. It is a win-win situation for the two boys: as any 1970s New York graffiti writer's success is measured in terms of the ubiquity of his tag, Mingus "gets to see his tag spread farther" (138). Dylan gets to "merge his identity with the black kid's, to lose his funkymusicwhiteboy geekdom in the illusion that he and his friend Mingus Rude are both Dose, no more and more less" (138). Soon Mingus will be tagging his own basement bedroom (205), while years later at Camden, Dylan and the visiting Arthur Lomb will tag the campus with "'authentic' Brooklyn graffiti, reproducing tags of FMD and DMD members" (396). Dylan's narration self-knowingly ironizes the idea that he is doing anything original or authentic in mimicking tags of graffiti crews well known in Brooklyn. Plus he realizes that stealing someone else's tag in New York City would have been a genuinely dangerous act.

The irony of graffiti as an art form, particularly in 1970s New York, is that its practitioners must remain anonymous since their work is illegal. At the same time, it is an activity founded on a competitive desire to make one's tag as visible as possible. It is simultaneously self-aggrandizing and self-negating. Peacock contrasts comics and graffiti on the basis that the former is fundamentally a private art form, created and consumed in solitude, while the latter is more public: "when Mingus unveils his new tag . . . what is revealed is the potential for a longing for secret identities to be united with public recognition and the reclamation of urban space."[14] Indeed many historians interpret New York graffiti as reflective of a desire to grant visibility, albeit in encoded ways, to marginalized people. What better way for Mingus to proclaim his own visibility and creative potency, then, than to use the enormous Dose tag, physically impossible without the magic ring's power of flight, on the side of the Brooklyn jail—an image that inscribes rebellious freedom onto an edifice standing for institutionalized disciplinary power. Eventually, Mingus and his tag will become so indistinguishable that in those third-person chapters of part 3 that describe Mingus's young adulthood, he is referred to not by name but as Dose.

If comics function as the popular art form that best mirrors Mingus and Dylan's friendship, and if graffiti is the art form in which Mingus finds his greatest creative power, then pop music is the art form most vital to Dylan's childhood. *The Fortress of Solitude* overflows with musical references, well before Dylan finds his vocation in adulthood in music journalism. Lethem has cast the music (and film and comics and television) references in *The Fortress of Solitude* as a doubling-down on the pop digressions of the novel that preceded it. He asks, "If one chapter in *Motherless Brooklyn* could take a lot of energy from describing a song by Prince, what would happen if every page of a six-hundred-page novel [*sic*] were bursting with references from music to film to street names?" (*Conv* 83). The most obvious musical reference points in *The Fortress of Solitude* are Dylan's and Mingus's equally symbolic names. Their names point to two of the most innovative and idiosyncratic popular musicians of the twentieth century, Bob Dylan and Charles Mingus. Both are masterful appropriators, incorporating and creatively reusing their influences. Both names, as Lethem employs them, work as racial signifiers also, though not in unbendingly strict ways, given that Bob Dylan's influences and collaborators include musicians of color while Charles Mingus's include white musicians. The plurality of these influences reflects the large extent to which both Dylan Ebdus and Mingus Rude take cultural cues from a multiplicity of cultural reference points around them.

Pop song lyrics also serve the vital purpose in part 1 of helping readers ground Dylan's childhood in time. In several scenes Dylan's friend Marilla sings pop songs on the street, enabling us to date events, if we recognize those lyrics and their moments of popularity, some instantly familiar and others more obscure (*TFoS* 7, 45, 66, 77, 91, 161). Additionally music taste signifies character traits in Dylan's mind. Barrett Rude Jr.'s records are fascinating and exotic, "the names and cover art windows to some distant world," while the AM-radio loves of the pre-Mingus-puppet Arthur Lomb, such as "Afternoon Delight" and "Convoy," are familiar but hopelessly boring (75, 157). At this point in the novel, Lethem depicts white music and black music as fairly separate spheres, but Dylan can navigate between the two, at least for now. Still, pop music can make him hyperaware of his whiteness, as in the ironized taunt "white boy" in Wild Cherry's "Play That Funky Music," which makes Dylan aware that "it was entirely possible that one song could destroy your life" (109). In other circumstances the right music can seem to erase racial difference, as in a positively idyllic Brooklyn street party scene. Lethem depicts very early Brooklyn hip-hop culture, including competing break-dancing crews and repeated uses of the classic Philly soul track "Love Is the Message" by MFSB on multiple turntables. Dylan has such a relaxed, "unhassled" night that he wonders whether "the ring has made him invisible. Maybe the ring has made him *black*. Who can say?" (165–68).

As Dylan ages and, more significantly, moves from Brooklyn public schools to Stuyvesant in Manhattan, his music tastes change, and the modes of racial identification attached to his listening get far more complex, personally and politically. In James Peacock's view, the fact that Dylan does not narrate part 1 does keep the depiction of childhood and adolescence from falling into easy nostalgia, but it also results in "a continuing resistance to the realities of racial separation and economic change, a desire to reduce such matters to pop representations, to appreciate their style, their form, not their political urgency."[15] Peacock implies there that pop representations and subcultural style within youth culture are apolitical, or at least that they lack the urgency of more serious or adult political interventions. For the pop-savvy reader, that is not the case. "Underberg" never implies that Dylan lacks a burgeoning sense of political awareness; instead it reveals that he comes to that awareness through pop-cultural artifacts, as do many pop-savvy readers and listeners. Lethem conveys this both in small details—for instance Dylan owning a record by the Specials, a racially integrated British ska band whose black-and-white checkerboard logo was meant as aggressively, if symbolically, antiracist—and in entire scenes.

When those scenes appear and reveal in fullest complexity the ideological arguments Dylan finds in his pop consumption, they tend to center around Dylan's interactions with his two closest non-Brooklyn friends from high school. Tim and Gabe, Dylan's geeky white buddies from Stuyvesant, are "harmless, pink-cheeked punks" who embrace punk aesthetics aggressively but a bit shallowly *(TFoS* 245). Tim buys "a point-studded dog collar" that fits together with "a simple snap," while Gabe, borrowing directly from the playbook of 1970s New York punks out to cultivate outsider personas via intentional shock, self-mutilates: "Gabe etched a tiny swastika on his forearm with a razor blade" (229). Tim's and Gabe's actions are indebted to the 1970s youth subcultural playbook as explained by the British sociologist Dick Hebdige in his landmark work *Subculture: The Meaning of Style* (1979). Youth subcultures, he argues, particularly punk, articulate their political standpoints implicitly by appropriating and recontextualizing signifiers that had been theretofore largely apolitical. For many British punks, Hebdige argues, reusing a garbage bag as a dress or a safety pin as a piece of jewelry can have truly resistant political purpose: "The safety pins and bin liners signified a relative material poverty which was either directly experienced and exaggerated or sympathetically assumed, and which in turn was made to stand for the spiritual paucity of everyday life."[16] Even wearing a swastika as Gabe does, though hardly an apolitical signifier in Dylan's lifetime, becomes in Hebdige's view not about proclaiming an allegiance to Nazism but about cheap shock value, a shallow political gesture but an intentional provocation that can be understood as political in the broadest possible sense of the term.[17] Lethem undercuts these possibilities, though, by introducing Tim and Gabe in terms of their relative privilege, at least compared to the Ebdus family: these two punk wannabes had previously been in New York private schools "until the year they switched to Stuyvesant to spare their parents the expense" (245). The implication here is that Tim and Gabe, unlike those youths described by Hebdige, do not originate punk style by fearlessly recontextualizing signifiers. Instead they are imitators, replicating the look faithfully, under its influence, seeing its desire to break free of the norm, and identifying with it enthusiastically.

Hebdige articulates these axes of cultural identification not through actual listening practices but instead through the visible activities of music-adjacent subcultures. For Dylan, though, personal and political identification has everything to do with one's listening choices, or put another way, what art one allows to bear the most influence in one's life. Dylan realizes that, young as it is, punk has already begun to splinter into subgenres or "related strands," as he puts it *(TFoS* 229). Foreshadowing his later vocation as a music journalist, Dylan finds the signifiers of the subgenres to be genuinely useful quasi-political categories: "Discerning their difference, articulating your precise relation, that was part of the point, a continuum of the now it was suddenly clear anyone could be placed on" (229). That said, confusion occurs when not everyone in the room knows how to read the signifiers that a subculture has redefined. Hebdige explains this, and Lethem depicts it directly.

Gabe has bought a "Ramonesian" leather jacket in an attempt to one-up Tim's dog collar, but a street tough promptly misinterprets it. When he confronts Gabe with "Think you're tough, you wanna fight me?" Gabe responds, "I actually *don't* think I'm tough, no" (*TFoS* 230). Lethem narrates, "This was a problem of codes, the self-loathing ironies of punkism not sufficiently conveyed yet to the Puerto Rican–gang quadrant of the universe" (230). When Gabe whines, "I'm just wearing it, it doesn't mean anything" (231), he really means *it doesn't mean what you think it does.* Lethem introduces the incident by explaining that the jacket "caused the only piece of trouble" these kids actually had as young punks in Manhattan (230). Dylan, Gabe, and Tim seem dismissive of any suggestion that they are in an unsafe place—"Fourteenth Street, First Avenue, they were scungy but populated," Lethem narrates (230)—but punk style itself still gets cast as potentially threatening given the perceived aggressiveness of its outsider pose. Later in Oakland, Dylan will be yoked on a bus while with a girlfriend (Lucinda Hoekke, incidentally, who will become a main character in *You Don't Love Me Yet* in one of Lethem's few cross-novel character reappearances). He is wearing "black-rimmed glasses" as an ironic affectation, "a Buddy Holly / Elvis Costello prop signifying rock hipness"—but only to him, as he apprehends that to the would-be yoker the glasses signify *muggable white dork* (410).

Some characters remain aware, though, that the outsider pose is just that: a pose. Having discovered and identified deeply with punk, Dylan trades in his mother's Creedence Clearwater Revival records, redolent of 1960s idealism, for the Clash's second album, a definitively punk document of negation and rebellion. Not long thereafter Dylan reflects on how the parting of ways in his and Mingus's changing musical tastes mirrors their gradual distancing from each other as friends. Where he and Mingus once could listen to soul and funk for hours, his Clash records are things "he'd never played for Mingus Rude because they embarrassed him on Dean Street, because he didn't know how" (*TFoS* 241). Lethem leaves that last clause unfinished, but he implies that Dylan would not know how to share punk, with its intellectualized and performative poses of outsiderness, with people on Dean Street, most of whom have lived their whole lives as outsiders in a more genuine, less performative fashion. Punk ironizes whatever it touches, Dylan realizes early. While watching a band of high school friends perform at CBGB, he describes the band's encore as "a comic cameo" in which the drummer sings Aretha Franklin's "Respect." The ironic punk cover of a beloved pop song may be a cliché gesture by now, but even when it is a relatively new concept circa 1980, Dylan sees it as a defense mechanism, a way in which a "pretty great song" "can be safely adored inside the ironical brackets of Upper West Side whiteboys playing the most famous punk club in the world" (260).

Two chapters earlier, though, Dylan evinced a bit more ambivalence about the racial politics of his listening choices. Dylan, Tim, and Gabe have just bought a twelve-inch of the Sugarhill Gang's "Rapper's Delight," a record that they find "inconceivably stupid and killingly funny" (*TFoS* 245). For Tim and Gabe, the very concept of hip-hop as a musical form is entirely new and is cast in cartoonish, comic terms: "They've never heard anyone rap before, anymore than they've met Fat Albert or Sanford & Son walking down the street" (246). But given his earlier presence at that instantly legendary block party, Dylan has already come into much closer contact with hip-hop culture than Tim and Gabe could ever imagine. Lethem adds, "If one of these three knows more, he's not telling" (245). Dancing and laughing about the track with his Stuyvesant pals, Dylan here fully aligns with Tim and Gabe (and by extension whiteness altogether), which necessitates a rejection of all things Dean Street, including Mingus. He is "just about finished leaving Dean Street, and Aeroman, behind. If this means avoiding the one who protected your ass all through junior high, the one you once ached to emulate, the one whose orbit you were happy just to swing in . . . that's a small price to pay for growing up, isn't it?" (246).

Later at Camden, Dylan will realize that this hyperawareness of the implications of his listening choices is not a quality shared by his classmates. At a party in a Camden dorm, the sharp lines he has seen separating black and white pop music seem to have disappeared, to judge from the playlist: "Rick James was followed by David Bowie, the Bowie by Orchestral Maneuvers in the Dark, and the OMD by Aretha Franklin" *(TFoS* 386). While his friends merely react to the music by dancing, Dylan intellectualizes his reaction. He sees his more carefree and privileged classmates dance and cannot get his head around "the suburban obliviousness of these white children to the intricate boundaries of race and music which were my inheritance and obsession" (386). Living as a member of the majority in some settings and the minority in others, Dylan brings to Camden a set of experiences and concerns that his all-majority-all-the-time white classmates do not fully grasp or, in this moment, even care to think about.

The chapter that includes the "Rapper's Delight" scene concludes with a pair of song lyrics, not signaled as such: "This ain't no party, this ain't no disco, this ain't no foolin' around. It's the end, the end of the seventies" *(TFoS* 246). The songs quoted, respectively, are "Life during Wartime" by Talking Heads (from *Fear of Music,* about which Lethem will later write a book in the acclaimed 33⅓ series) and "Do You Remember Rock 'n' Roll Radio?" by the Ramones. These lines' air of finality, coming at chapter's end, implies that Dylan has conclusively rejected black music in favor of white, his Dean Street friends in favor of his Stuyvesant friends, and eventually Brooklyn in favor of Camden College. Dylan overhearing Marilla's shouts of lyrics to Jackson Five and Chaka Khan singles is out. Dylan laughing at "Rapper's Delight" while quoting punk and new wave bands is in.

A handful of other key scenes mark significant moments in Dylan's coming-of-age in a curiously tentative fashion, each emphasizing how Dylan gradually pulls away from Dean Street while coming to realize how different he is from his neighbors. One such moment occurs when Robert Woolfolk runs into Dylan at a pizzeria and commands a younger kid, "a small version of himself," to steal Dylan's pizza (*TFoS* 195). Dylan sees the reticence in Robert's protégé, recognizes this as a case of "master instructing apprentice" (195), and calmly eats the pizza anyway, understanding that if Robert intervenes, he is implicitly acknowledging that he has failed to train his follower to yoke properly. For the first time, Dylan resists the yoke (and from his childhood nemesis, no less), but the only thing that has changed in this interaction is Dylan's age. He remains ever the "whiteboy," though, still marked by racial difference and getting any authority he has on the street from age alone, his new status as one who has not only survived on Dean Street but also thrived there. When he is in high school, Dylan notices a much younger Dean Street child drawing a "primitive botched skully board" on the pavement for a street game, hears him call Dylan "honky," and cracks up "laughing at the sweetness of it" (222). As Dylan gains confidence and experience throughout his teenage years, he gradually redefines New York less as a site of limitation and more as a site of possibility. The place and time "are not about urban decay, fiscal shortfalls, and the limitations of the civil rights movement. They are the world of his youth, at once frightening and exhilarating, perplexing and charged with meaning."[18] Indeed, Hughes takes pains to point out that during the sometimes truly scary summer of 1977, a season defined by widespread fear of the Son of Sam serial killer as well as the enormous New York blackout and the looting that followed it, Dylan is safely ensconced in Vermont, thanks to the give-city-kids-a-rural-experience organization called the Fresh Air Fund, and has a crush on the daughter of his host family.[19] There he will continue to find ways to trade on the act of exoticizing his upbringing: he tells his Vermont crush, "My best friend is black," knowing that he is playing a card that makes him sound, in that moment, more mysterious than he really is (172).

Six chapters and a few years after the pizzeria scene, though, Dylan's sense of his own difference from the rest of the street, as well as his growing detachment from Mingus and Arthur, comes through as he buys Mingus's comic book collection. Mingus and Arthur, heavy cocaine users by now, plan to buy their own supply to resell for a profit, so Dylan consents to "take those comics off [their] hands" (*TFoS* 280). He pays three hundred dollars in precollege summer job earnings, casually throwing the cash to his old friends as if to convey "how puny the sum was to him. This was a demonstration to all three of them, as representatives of Gowanus, that Dylan was no longer of this place" (282). The invocation of Gowanus is important there, as a reminder that this trio's uneasy friendship dates back to the earliest days of Dean Street's gentrification. This scene, however, serves as an informal end to Dylan's childhood, punctuated by his exit from Mingus's bedroom with his friend's old comics and, impulsively, an Afro pick, which Dylan grabs on the way out. "Dylan was like the garbage man of their entire youth, come at last," our narrator says (280), emphasizing how little value the comics now have as a marker of friendship. They are worthwhile now only in trade value as Mingus and Arthur try to scrape together drug money. The next time Dylan visits Mingus, the idyll of his Dean Street youth will end even more definitively.

In that scene Dylan comes to ask Mingus to return the ring. During the visit Dylan does a line of coke for the first time, with Barrett present and partaking also, and the drugs serve as an odd bonding force, now that comics can no longer do so. Dylan compares this visit and its unlikely normality to a scene from "an alternate life, one where he'd never abandoned the block, never quit visiting this house" (*TFoS* 289). Suddenly Barrett Sr. walks in on them midsnort and accuses Barrett Jr. of "corrupting the morals of another neighbor child" (290). As the confrontation between father and son builds, Barrett Sr. produces a gun, and Mingus commands Dylan to leave, "protecting him still" (291). Part 1 ends with Dylan barely outside the Rude home when he hears a gunshot.

The full story of what transpires in the Rude home does not get explained in full until the end of part 2 of the novel, titled "Liner Note." Though only thirteen pages long, it is a hugely important piece of *The Fortress of Solitude* because it is the only example readers get of Dylan Ebdus's work as an adult. A music journalist, Dylan has taken to writing liner notes for box sets and remastered CDs for Remnant Records, a reissue label. His liner note for a reissue of Barrett Rude's greatest hits is heartfelt but suffers from some overly academic flourishes, such as an epigraph from Brian Eno, and some purple-prose quirks such as a few paragraphs written in the second person. His employer at Remnant will later tell Dylan in a phone conversation that it is "not your best work," explaining that the essay "reads like you were avoiding something" (*TFoS* 379). For his own part, when Dylan gives Barrett a copy of the reissue, he immediately regrets how he has characterized Barrett's poststardom years, particularly the dismissive ending to Rude's capsule biography: "For what it's worth the man is still alive" (306, 435).

Peacock reads "Liner Note" as Dylan's crafty and dubious attempt to retell Barrett Rude's story in a fashion that lets Dylan claim some ownership of anything good that he ever saw in his childhood Brooklyn. Accomplishing that, though, requires selective memory as well as the (admittedly limited) power that comes with Dylan's success as a music writer. In this interpretation, Dylan's essay about Barrett becomes "a devious act of remediation and of appropriation. His name, now officially sanctioned, allows him to re-author Barrett Rude and, by association, Mingus, Court Street, and the 'authentic' Gowanus of his youth."[20] Indeed, Dylan's own writing casts youthful experiences as the only valuable ones, as he describes how Barrett's music "lead[s] nowhere, though, if not back to your own neighborhood. To the street where you live. To things you left behind. And *that's* what you need, what you needed all along" (*TFoS* 306). Part 3 of *The Fortress of Solitude* consists largely of Dylan coming to realize that he needs to take his own advice.

Like many other moments in Lethem's work (for example, revealing the dead man's hand at the end of *Motherless Brooklyn*), "Liner Note" has added impact for readers who are in the know about certain bits of cultural lore. Lethem's ideal reader of *The Fortress of Solitude* knows his or her pop music history as well as Dylan Ebdus does, and by the end of "Liner Note," a pop-savvy reader will identify Barrett Rude Jr. to be an analogue of Motown great Marvin Gaye. Both are soul singers who successfully cross over onto the pop charts with huge singles before leaving pop behind for more socially conscious music in the early 1970s (in Gaye's case, *What's Going On;* in Rude's case, *In Your Neighborhood*). Both experience messy public divorces and release angry music about the experience (Gaye: *Here, My Dear;* Rude: *Take It, Baby*) and deal with cocaine addictions soon thereafter. As the pieces of Rude's story fall ever more into place in a way that closely resembles Gaye's story, and as Lethem's reader knows that someone was just shot in the Rude home at the end of part 1, the pop-savvy reader expects to read that Rude's life has been ended by his father, as Gaye's was in 1984. Instead the revelation at the end of "Liner Note" that Mingus shot Barrett Sr., not, as Lethem has set readers up to expect, that Barrett Sr. has shot Barrett Jr., gets much of its impact from the shock of Lethem's decision to rewrite a fairly familiar tragic story from contemporary pop lore.

This scene, begun at the end of part 1 and not fully explained until the end of part 2, signals a rather definitive end to Dylan's childhood, chronologically if not psychologically. As part 3 opens, Dylan is an adult, he lives in Berkeley with his (not at all coincidentally, African American) girlfriend Abby, and he and Abby are fighting. In the midst of their argument over Dylan's moodiness, Dylan stammers, "My childhood is the only part of my life that wasn't, uh, overwhelmed by my childhood" (*TFoS* 319). He is clearly thinking of the scene that ends part 1. That is signaled by the fact that Dylan's comment is bookended by a digression in his argument with Abby over why Dylan owns an Afro pick. Of course it is the pick that Dylan took from Mingus as he bought Mingus's comic book collection in their last visit before the shooting. For Abby, it is one of many examples of Dylan fetishizing blackness, or as she puts it in describing his personal treasury of pop music, with its considerable presence of blues and classic soul, "the Ebdus collection of *sad black folks*" (317). Dylan's response is cutting: "I guess I have to listen to this shit because you don't feel black enough, Abby. Because you grew up riding ponies in the suburbs" (319), just as Mingus grew up playing youth football in the suburbs. Abby retorts that Dylan's Afro pick told her where she stood from the first time she saw Dylan's bedroom: "I said to myself, Abby, this man is collecting you for the color of your skin" (319). What Abby might not know is that Dylan has fetishized blackness for quite a while already.

In appearing to "collect" signifiers of African American experience, Dylan seeks to build a self-created but rather tenuous identity every bit as much as Lionel in *Motherless Brooklyn* attempts to play the part of the hard-boiled private eye, or every bit as much as the young Arthur Lomb does in becoming a "Mingus-puppet." Dylan comes to realize, though, that unlike Lionel, his youthful performances contained more than just a touch of an uncomfortable element of minstrelsy. "I earned my stripe at Camden by playing a walking artifact of the ghetto," he recalls (*TFoS* 389). Whereas in high school at Stuyvesant he had cultivated an air of preppiness as his defensive facade, he realizes at Camden that this affectation does not play as such "to those who'd actually been to prep school" (389). He picks up instead a "shtick" that amounts to being "a cartoon of Mingus," "a splendid container for my self-loathing, and for my hostility toward my classmates" (389). He feigns complete ignorance of anything that or anyone who might be associated with wealth, takes up certain elements of early 1980s black style (such as a Kangol cap and the all-purpose greeting "yo"), and admits that this performed identity made him popular on campus, though perhaps more as a curiosity than anything else. The French sociologist Pierre Bourdieu has argued that personal preferences in matters of taste and style often double as attempts to differentiate oneself positively from one's peers in order to garner the cultural capital that comes with distinction.[21] In admitting that his performance of "inner-city knowledge" is "a trick of flirting," Dylan reveals that he is performing his difference from the mass of Camden students, and he earns himself considerable cultural capital in doing so (387). Arthur's visit with Dylan at Camden complicates things, though. On one level, Arthur's self-presentation confirms Dylan's story. On another level, Arthur's self-presentation trumps Dylan's story. "Arthur struck them as something *real*," Dylan explains, given "his baggy jeans and fat laces and clumsy patois, his constant references to rap and graffiti" (395). Arthur's performances of black style somehow read as less forced than Dylan's, presumably because Arthur is not attending the most expensive college in America.

Dylan's faux nouveau riche fantasy ends, however, when he is caught on campus with cocaine, and Abraham finds out via a letter from Camden's president, explaining that Dylan may be allowed to reapply for his scholarship after a term's suspension. Dylan's reality, that the Ebdus family cannot really afford Camden, is implied to be the real and unspoken reason for his suspension. Having earlier established that Camden sometimes looks the other way from its students' decadences, Dylan now points out that while Camden "could, and would, protect itself from the Vermont narcotics squad," it is also the college's prerogative to "protect itself from me and Arthur Lomb" (*TFoS* 405). With no return to Camden in his future, Dylan feels as if he may as well never have left Brooklyn. He chooses to go as far away from Brooklyn as he can, all the way to Berkeley, California, to attend college and essentially to stay. He is still living in Berkeley when the adult Dylan starts narrating part 3, arguing with Abby while getting ready to go see his father in Los Angeles at the sci-fi convention where he will be honored. There Dylan will learn that the convention organizer's research on Abraham has uncovered Rachel's last known address, in Bloomington, Indiana. That revelation, however shadowy in its moment of disclosure, sends Dylan on a trip into his past, starting with Brooklyn. Inevitably, Dylan the music collector frames his decision in Beatlesque terms: "I had to get back to where I once belonged" (381).

Making sense of this personal past requires Dylan to retrace his steps to once-familiar places and reconnect with once-familiar friends, to be sure. It also requires him to articulate more fully his relationship to the artworks that have been formative influences on him. It is first important to realize that Dylan has understood himself as an artistically inclined individual from childhood—in watching football with Mingus and Barrett, he chooses the Minnesota Vikings "on helmet aesthetics" (*TFoS* 72)—largely because of the constant presence of Abraham's art-making in his own home. But that does not mean that Dylan is an artist. Dylan's father has given up traditional figurative painting for experimental filmmaking; he paints, like his hero Stan Brakhage, directly onto celluloid. To support this work, he starts painting psychedelic covers for a series of sci-fi novels. Abraham's old art teacher and mentor gets him the job, sadly bemoaning all the while his perceived lack of originality in the contemporary art and literary worlds: "The writers don't write, they stand on-stage and play with themselves instead, emulating Mailer and Ginsberg. We've lost a generation. . . . Tradition's kaput. Nothing's good enough, not since Warhol, that schmuck" (80). He does not quite say that it has all been done, but he is skeptical that much more art of substance will be made in the future. Much later an excerpt of Abraham's still-unfinished film gets screened at the sci-fi convention where Abraham is a guest of honor, now that Abraham has earned for his years of work a level of acclaim in the sci-fi community that he finds truly bewildering. In describing his own work to the convention audience, Abraham dismisses the idea that he displays any originality either, casting himself as an essentially imitative artist too. He sees himself as mimicking "Ernst, Tanguy, Matta, Kandinsky. Once in a while, the early Pollock or Rothko. If I've accomplished one thing, it's been to give a rough education in contemporary painting, or what was contemporary painting in 1950. . . . It's derivative, every last brushstroke. All quoted" (345–46). In this explanation, Abraham casts himself as operating under the heavy influence of the greats of modern surrealist and abstract expressionist art.

Except for his myriad re-creations of the graffiti tag that Mingus actually originated, the only actual visual art Dylan has produced is one frame in Abraham's film, which he created in secret, alone in Abraham's studio. He does not know whether or not Abraham ever discovered the tiny forgery, nor does he know if Abraham retained or removed that frame. Like Dylan's borrowing of Mingus's tag, this act of creation is really an act of imitation. Dylan borrowed Mingus's tag earlier because he has such a "gift for mimicry," "honed in a thousand Spirograph spirals" *(TFoS* 138). Dylan's imitation is childlike apprentice work at best, far removed from the sort of creative appropriation Lethem will celebrate in "The Ecstasy of Influence." Dylan calls that single frame of film "my sole contribution" (361), and while he means that it is his only direct contribution to his father's work, the phrasing implies that he is aware of how limited his powers of perceived originality really are. Or, as Dylan puts it after he realizes that graffiti has started appearing all over Brooklyn, right under his nose, and he needs to catch up, "Most things had happened some time before Dylan came along" (72–73). Like Abraham's teacher, he says not that it has *all* been done but that it has *mostly* been done.

Influence and fandom first come together in *The Fortress of Solitude* when Abraham takes a still quite young Dylan to hear his primary artistic influence, Stan Brakhage, "a great man, a beautiful man" (*TFoS* 139), speak as part of a panel at Cooper Union. The other panelists exhibit the anger of critics who have convinced themselves of their otherwise unrecognized genius: they speak in "spiky, resentful tones" that imply "that they alone understood the filmmaker's work" (140). The gathering begins to go off the rails as some in attendance shout questions at the panelists out of turn, and the tension in the room goes away only when Brakhage brings order to the proceedings in a Q&A period, "as the panelists were rendered equal to the audience of Brakhage's authority" (141). Abraham leaves frustrated that he has not been able to share with Dylan any sense of what he has been trying to achieve with his own Brakhage-influenced work.

In part 3 Abraham will have a similar experience when he is honored at a California sci-fi convention. Abraham's work has become coveted in the sci-fi community, as we learn that there is now "an online zine called Ebdus Collector, dedicated to the purchase of the rare original painted boards" that became paperback covers *(TFoS* 342). Abraham too is part of a contentious panel, where he insists that despite the sci-fi community's interest in his work, he thinks of himself as a failure, acknowledging that his real work is his film. Sidney Blumlein, one of the first people in sci-fi publishing to hire Abraham, explains to the audience, calmly if a little dismissively, that Abraham is an artist, not a fan. His commonsense attitude sounds quite akin to Lethem's attitude toward Philip K. Dick: "We're fans, our interests begin in the pulp-magazine tradition, however we might like to hope we've elevated it" (344). It is no accident, then, that Abraham's new girlfriend Francesca identifies Blumlein to Dylan as "the only one [present on the panel] your father respects" (343). When asked what he thinks of the sci-fi field that he has spent much of a career keeping at arm's length, he calls it "a bohemian demimonde, like any other" (346). The phrase sounds dismissive, and Dylan will reclaim its positive possibilities in the novel's final pages, but there is a generosity in Abraham's equation of this subculture's quirks with any other subculture's quirks. Perhaps he remembers that seated at the feet of Brakhage, he acted much as the sci-fi fans do here.

Lethem's relationship to the sci-fi fan community is complicated, as the convention scenes in *The Fortress of Solitude* imply. Lethem respects and affirms the enthusiasm these fans bring to the discussion of the art they so love. At the same time, he faults them for a dismissive and reactionary attitude toward non–sci-fi art that he casts as the equal and opposite reaction to the mainstream literary community's dismissal of sci-fi. One metaphor, developed over the course of multiple essays in *The Ecstasy of Influence,* characterizes the alternative literary community that is sci-fi writers, publishers, and readers as "the Radisson bar." The essay "What I Learned at the Science-Fiction Convention" introduces the image by characterizing a sci-fi convention as "a floating opera" that alights for mere days at a time at one of many conference-hosting hotels, where much of the real building of relationships and exchange of ideas happens not at official panels but in the hotel bar (*TEoI* 68). Lethem uses this idiosyncratic running metaphor for several purposes. First, it emphasizes what Lethem sees as a genuine sense of camaraderie among this group of like-minded outsiders. Second, he uses it to explain how some pieces of the worldview he associates with sci-fi have effectively bled into a wide variety of mainstream culture, in both high-art and pop-cultural circles. Third, he animates it in greater detail later when he critiques the aggression and learned victimhood of a certain kind of entrenched artistic outsider—an unattractive character trait shared in different ways by both Ebdus men in *The Fortress of Solitude* and taken to an extreme in Perkus Tooth in *Chronic City.* Lethem admits that he is guilty too: "I'd surely been enacting my own inversion of privilege by insisting on my genre scars: I'd be an outer-borough kid who'd taken the subway to the big literary city, and had possibly also hopped the turnstiles on his way" (70). That said, he admits that in the Radisson bar, he has "made lifelong friends" and that despite his successes in the literary mainstream, "the conversation never really got better than the talk in the bar of the Radisson" (70, 430).

As odd as Dylan finds the sci-fi convention (and as much as he is clearly there only out of love for his father), he recognizes that this fan subculture is really no different from any number of other subcultures, including those in his own profession of music journalism. He compares this convention to "panels at the South by Southwest conference or the CMJ [Music Marathon], which were no less self-congratulatorily marginal" *(TFoS* 347). In a prophetic moment that foresees even further fragmentation of entertainment into niche media for niche audiences, Dylan pictures "a world dotted with conferences, convocations, and 'Cons' of all types, each an engine for converting feelings of inferiority and self-loathing into their opposites" (347). In this vision of the world, the supportive communities would be good, Dylan thinks, but the insularity less so.

The novel's first reference to the communal impulses of music journalists such as Dylan appears in part 1, when Lethem describes a (fictional) jammy funk tune that barely made the airplay charts in 1978. Its only real claim to semifame is the uncredited appearance of Barrett Rude Jr., attempting a comeback. It was not a smash hit, but "nerd connoisseurs were left to savor it later, to champion or slag it in their endless tinny dialogue" *(TFoS* 201). Right away record collectors and music hounds, the subculture of which the adult Dylan will be fully part in part 3, are cast as geeky and irritating. That said, younger collectors and fans, still finding their way into their cultural obsessions, are depicted as approaching their enthusiasms with appropriate youthful energy. Mingus explains that his father has such a huge record collection that he has access to "all the cuts them DJs can't even find" (204). Tim and Gabe, quoting Monty Python films and early *Saturday Night Live,* adroitly wield their "vocal graffiti of impersonations" (218). These enthusiasms have their limits, though,

Lethem reveals. While manically talking music and movies with some Manhattan friends (and playing around with a pet theory that any group of four fictional characters represents a set of archetypal personae comparable to the Beatles), Dylan realizes that this sort of talk is no way to ingratiate himself to the opposite sex: "To the ironized, reference-peppered palaver which comprises Dylan's only easy mode of talk, former prep-school girls have frequently proved deaf as cats" (265).

By part 3 Dylan is in full curatorial mode, having worked as a DJ, become a serious record collector, and written liner notes. Having earned his own college radio show at Berkeley, he reports rediscovering the classic soul of his childhood in the station's archives and eventually becoming "a vinyl hawk, scouring record shops for out-of-print LPs, studying them with Talmudic intensity" *(TFoS* 408). Since much of this music had not yet made it to CDs, he claims, it felt "entirely my own" (408). All the while the theme song for Dylan's show is a classic new wave track, Ian Dury's "Reasons to Be Cheerful, Part 3." Dylan calls it "a Monty Pythonesque white rap" (407), but it might also be the single pop song that best sums up the curatorial impulse. Dylan calls it "my anthem" (407). A nifty list tune that includes witty Gilbert and Sullivan–esque rhymes, Dury's song, like Lethem's work, pays tribute to a wide variety of cultural loves: Buddy Holly, the Marx Brothers, Salvador Dali, John Coltrane, and Woody Allen, to name only a few of Dury's many name-checks.

Fortuitously, he is also living in the perfect time for such a culturally literate influence hound to find curatorial work: in the 1990s there was an upswing of interest in all things retro, and Dylan points out that the hottest new radio format is a mix of classic R & B and disco called "Jammin' Oldies" *(TFoS* 321). Mingus is not immune to this rebirth of interest in past music: in the recap of his adult life between the shooting and his current incarceration, he occasionally looks through his father's old records and finds "treasures moldering in disuse" (482). For his own part, though, Dylan's work for Remnant Records is not always about brilliant rediscoveries. While he reports having some successes, Dylan goes into the most detail in describing his truly strange plan for *Liner Notes: The Box Set.* Having fallen in love with "the uncanny found poetry" sometimes to be found on the backs or gatefolds of old records, he envisions a box set, packaged like a multirecord set of LPs, consisting only of reproductions of significant liner notes. "That it might be regarded as a disappointment to find not a single note of actual music" there does not occur to Dylan (414). Dylan ruefully admits that it was a bad idea, a transparent attempt to place the music critic on the same plane as the musician. He speaks dismissively of the plan, but as deeply misguided as the concept is (though it could make a great printed anthology in book form with Dylan as editor), at least Dylan desires to put something into the world in a form never seen before, however odd. Lethem's later and fuller critique of the curatorial impulse in *Chronic City* will center on Perkus Tooth's inability (or more likely, lack of will) to create anything remotely new at all.

Dylan has far more interest in reproducing the past than in building a new future, as the entire concept of *Liner Notes: The Box Set* implies. In his hotel room after visiting Mingus in prison but before sneaking *back* into prison with the magic invisibility ring to break Mingus out, Dylan muses that he has spent his adulthood "flinching from what mattered most—not California, dummy, but Brooklyn. Not Camden College, but Intermediate School 293. Not Talking Heads, but Al Green" *(TFoS* 448). The music he loved in high school and college now looks to him like artifacts of his failed attempt at upward mobility via Camden. He later concludes that such music stands for all he "had to refuse in favor of soul, in favor of Barrett Rude Junior and his defiant, unsubtle pain" (509–10). Not long after seeing the adult Arthur Lomb in his restaurant, Dylan runs into his childhood friend Marilla, who still lives on Dean Street. As they catch up briefly, and Marilla reminds Arthur that she knew Dylan before Arthur did, "claims of provenance poured from us" (433). "Maybe I'd first found it on Dean Street," Dylan thinks, "my rage for authenticity" (434). At first it may sound as though Dylan is back to his old ways here, invoking a rediscovered love of Al Green and Barrett Rude as just a new chapter in his fetishizing of blackness. At the same time, Lethem suggests that Dylan grows ever more aware of how cheap and deceitful nostalgia can be.

While I do not argue that Dylan has given up fetishizing blackness entirely, part 3 opens and closes with contrasting statements from Dylan that reflect some growth over a short period of time. As a result, Peacock argues, part 3 dramatizes Dylan's rejection "of blackness itself as a utopia, a construction that tends to ignore social realities."[22] In the second paragraph of "Prisonaires," Dylan matter-of-factly observes, "I loved having a black girlfriend, and I loved Abby," paired comments that, in this moment, Dylan most definitely means in that order *(TFoS* 312). Near the novel's end, while visiting Mingus in prison, Dylan hears Mingus admit that he too had yoked a white kid before. Mingus describes making "the mean face," which Dylan registers as little more than a "scowl, yet the volt of panic it struck in me was one of my life's companions" (492). His next question reveals a broader understanding of racial difference than he has yet evinced anywhere else in the novel: "What age is a black boy when he learns he's scary?" (492). In those eleven words, Dylan expresses a belated realization that even as he shares a common childhood neighborhood with Mingus and even as their different races do not automatically lead them to predetermined futures, their different races do lead them to be viewed differently by much of the world. Mingus and Dylan could once trade on the prejudices of others as a team, letting department store employees trail Mingus while Dylan shoplifted the spray paint for a night's graffiti writing (145–48). But now Mingus's conversation with Dylan in prison gives him a chance to explain to Dylan how the lived realities of race have not been the same for him as they have for his friend.

Put another way, when a white woman asks the young Dylan, "Hey, kid? Something wrong?" after seeing him hanging out with Mingus and Robert, she is expressing concern, as hugely misguided (and to Dylan, humiliating) as her action is *(TFoS* 123–25). When Mingus yokes a white kid in Brooklyn Heights, others think him terrifying. By novel's end, Dylan begins to understand this.

One surprising note of building consensus in the critical conversation about *The Fortress of Solitude* is that for all of its magical flying rings, digressions about punk rock, and occasional romanticization of lonely artists, the book has already begun to take its place as one of the young century's most important political novels. Evan Hughes refers to Lethem's Brooklyn in *Motherless Brooklyn* and *The Fortress of Solitude* (primarily the latter) as "a laboratory of democracy that the suburbs cannot replicate."[23] He does not stop at emphasizing Lethem's interest in questions of political equality; instead he places Lethem firmly in the long tradition of American urban writers working to make sense of how best to put national ideals into practice. Hughes places Lethem in the lineage of Walt Whitman, "dramatizing the weird tumult and diversity of the American city" and spotlighting "the egalitarian poetry in what happens close to the ground."[24] Similarly, Samuel Cohen makes a strong case for *The Fortress of Solitude* as a novel that "connect[s] the past to a future whose tenuousness places it at the center of the contemporary American historical imagination."[25] Matt Godbey's reading is not as laudatory, as he faults Lethem for "only allud[ing] to the black perspective" and marginalizing Mingus's perspective on gentrification,[26] but the questions he asks and the issues he raises, of race, privilege, and narrative representation of Others, are comparable to those of Hughes.

In addition Cohen offers an eloquent defense of "Prisonaires," the final section of *The Fortress of Solitude,* which many reviewers critiqued for allegedly lacking the perceived vibrancy of the novel's depiction of Dylan and Mingus's shared youth. As Ray Davis puts it, Lethem's "formally-dictated break" from the artist figures in part 1 to the critic figures of parts 2 and 3 "created genuine reader distress."[27] Cohen explains that part 3 is all about Dylan attempting to come to terms with his childhood without fully succeeding. As a result, the work becomes a historical novel that is radically open-ended; its first part depicts the past with loads of nostalgically sensual detail, while the following parts show Dylan reflecting on that past without ever suggesting that he has completely made sense of his past—or that he necessarily ever will. More specifically, Cohen contrasts the open-endedness of Lethem's ending against the more traditional novelistic closure available to readers of Jeffrey Eugenides's *Middlesex* (2002). In *The Fortress of Solitude* the past can neither be fully assimilated into the present nor severed from the present. In other words, as soon as Dylan tries to account for his aimless early adulthood *on top of* his distant childhood past, he finds himself with a far more difficult task. Or as Cohen puts it, "Dylan's dilemmas . . . are harder to resolve if he figures in all of his life rather than just a distant, severed past."[28]

As the novel ends, Dylan's attempt to come to terms with his past remains incomplete. Having discovered earlier that the ring's power has mysteriously switched from flight to invisibility, Dylan uses that invisibility to get into the prison where both Mingus and Robert are incarcerated. Mingus refuses to take the ring from Dylan, telling him to give it to Robert instead. Unaware that the superpower has shifted, Robert dies when he jumps from a tower in the prison yard. From there Dylan drives to Bloomington, where he finds Isabel Vendle's nephew Croft, Rachel's onetime lover and companion on an Indiana commune. He offers Dylan the typewriter on which she wrote the Running Crab postcards; he declines. The final scene of the novel, a flashback to Abraham driving Dylan home from Camden after his expulsion, depicts a "motion half-completed . . . not something to be completed but rather what all motion through time is—not something to be finished, as if that were possible, but something that continues onward, turning present into past, heading blindly into the future."[29] Not only that, but in that moment Dylan is listening to a piece of music, the Brian Eno album *Another Green World,* that he loves because it evokes a "middle space," "a bohemian demimonde, a hippie dream" *(TFoS* 509). Lethem uses the phrase "bohemian demimonde" three more times in the *Conversations* volume of interviews, and it shows up once more in *The Ecstasy of Influence.* It is introduced in *The Fortress of Solitude* via Abraham's dismissal of the insular subculture of the sci-fi convention (346), but Dylan views it more favorably. Cohen appreciates the novel's ending for its open-endedness, leaving Dylan fully in neither past nor present. In these final pages, Dylan appreciates his own unusual situation too, finding an odd comfort, while in transit, in a middle space that conflates past and present as well.

For many readers, *The Fortress of Solitude* represents a giant leap forward in Lethem's body of work. In certain regards unmistakably autobiographical and more committed than any previous Lethem work to depicting the specific textures of a real place, the novel does introduce some features to Lethem's work that are genuinely new. At the same time, it is a continuation and further development of some of *Motherless Brooklyn*'s key features, particularly Lethem's growing willingness to deemphasize plot advancement occasionally in favor of detailed digressions on cultural artifacts that have influenced him or his characters. In drawing connections from *Motherless Brooklyn* to *The Fortress of Solitude,* here Lethem is his own best critic. Part 3 of *The Fortress of Solitude,* "Prisonaires," has surprising resonances with *Motherless Brooklyn:*

> It's almost exactly the same length. Both begin with an adult narrator introducing himself in the midst of conflict where his "other" abandons him. Frank Minna is killed in the first chapter of *Motherless;* Abby splits in the first chapter of "Prisonaires." This loss sends each character careening through a story that, in its "present," takes only a few days. *Motherless* takes four days from the first chapter, and the second half of *Fortress* takes five or six days. Both are absolutely hectic with plot and epiphanies, and both make room for an approximately hundred-page flashback to childhood, in which we learn what is truly at stake in the present. In fact, both end in cross-country car trips and climax at these rather non sequitur locations—Maine and Indiana—where the main character learns the secret-hiding-within-the-secret of the book. Both secrets have to do with the past life of an important female character at a bohemian enclave. The similarities go on and on. (*Conv* 62)

What is new in *The Fortress of Solitude,* though, is the presence of characters who not only live under the influence of the art they love but create as well. Lionel Essrog lived in Raymond Chandler's world; Abraham Ebdus and Barrett Rude Jr. and, to a lesser extent perhaps, Dylan and Mingus work to shape their own world in their acts of creation. When Dylan describes reading liner notes aloud on his college radio show, he says he "learned that to find one's art is to kill time dead with a single shot. I felt akin to Abraham" (*TFoS* 408). Abraham, Dylan concludes, had a "better idea" than Rachel all along since his painting let him "carve the middle space on a daily basis, alone in his room" (510). Art-making in *The Fortress of Solitude* can practically stop time, it is so powerful and connectional. At its best, passionate enjoyment of art can do the same. Looking ahead to *Chronic City,* Lethem will reveal the tragedy that can happen when critical and artistic types use the power of taste-making and the ecstasy of influence not to forge connections but to avoid them.

CHAPTER 4

Chronic City

Ecstatic Appreciation and Its Discontents

There could be few more appropriate locations for *Chronic City* to open than in the New York offices of the Criterion Collection, a well-regarded and widely beloved maker of high-end DVD releases of artistically significant films. Lethem has brought his critical eye to Criterion projects in the past: he has recorded commentary for the Criterion edition of Nicholas Ray's *Bigger than Life* and contributed essays to reissues of Preston Sturges's *Unfaithfully Yours* and Robert Siodmak's *The Killers.* As is to be expected perhaps, all three are genre films (melodrama, romantic comedy, and noir, respectively), though ones with far darker worldviews than they appear to present at first glance. At the Criterion offices, *Chronic City*'s narrator Chase Insteadman has his first chance encounter with Perkus Tooth, and the two fall into an intense if sometimes combative friendship, becoming another one of Lethem's dynamic male duos. If *The Fortress of Solitude* is about the lifelong act of locating (and relocating) one's self through imaginative identification with popular culture, *Chronic City* reveals what happens when that same impulse, joyful appreciation of culture, gets taken to its most logical extreme. It is a book about fandom gone wild to the point that it becomes debilitating.

Before a discussion of *Chronic City,* though, some of Lethem's works published between *The Fortress of Solitude* and *Chronic City* are particularly worthy of attention. During those years Lethem published three books in particular that develop some of Lethem's recurring points of interest. *Men and Cartoons* (2004) is a collection of short stories that trade heavily in the blurring of lines between literary fiction and pulpy midcentury genre work. Even the hardcover dust jacket gets in on this charming retro act: its back cover presents itself as a parody of the arrays of mail-order offers taking up the back pages of old-school comic books. Capsule summaries of the volume's nine stories appear in the guise of advertisements for novelty goods, situated among authentic-looking novelty ads for items such as switchblades, sea monkeys, and fake dog excrement.

A few recurring ideas in Lethem's fiction appear in the book. A key scene in "The Vision" takes place in a room bounded by "walls lined with CDs, laser discs, and books, many of them expensive museum catalogues, compendiums of film stills, photo-essays from boutique imprints" (*Men and Cartoons* 10). Half living space and half personal archive, this physical testimony to personal taste could be the adult Dylan Ebdus's room filled with music in *The Fortress of Solitude* or the apartment of Perkus Tooth, soon to appear in *Chronic City*. Perkus's writer-critic-curator role is adumbrated by the narrator of "Planet Big Zero," who draws a monthly comic "for a free music magazine produced by a record-store chain," which regularly features characters who "have a stupid adventure and review a new CD by a major rock act" (82). Most important to a full understanding of Lethem's aesthetic, though, is "Super Goat Man," which presents a failed superhero as symbolic of the failed utopian promise of the 1960s counterculture.

James Peacock reads the climax of "Super Goat Man," in which the title character is unable to save a drunk college student from a fatal fall from a clock tower, as a critique of the American mythology of the superhero.[1] At the same time, though, the story's narrator meets Super Goat Man when the superhero is a guest at his hippie parents' commune, and Super Goat Man's status as an *ex*-superhero gets special attention. This character "exists as both an ontological reality and as a fiction, specifically a comic book superhero. . . . This fact is simply taken for granted,"[2] much as readers are never really meant to question the veracity of the magic ring in *The Fortress of Solitude*. Ever the chronicler of his characters' reading material, Lethem's narrator notes that works by Mailer, Pynchon, and Sergei Eisenstein are visible on the bookshelves during his first meeting with Super Goat Man; furthermore the books make such an impression that he owns up to "later attempt[ing] to read each of the three at college, succeeding only with the Mailer" (*Men and Cartoons* 123). Super Goat Man will later have a short stint, in "1981, the dawn of Reagan," as a faculty member at the narrator's New England liberal arts college (shades of both Dylan Ebdus's and Lethem's experiences there), teaching a class called "Dissidence and Desire: Marginal Heroics in American Life 1955–1975," with Timothy Leary prominently featured on the syllabus (127). Lethem reminds us that by the boom days of neoconservatism, Super Goat Man's past radicalism is a museum piece: the college moves to "enshrine what had once been at the vigorous center of the culture in the harmless pantheon of academia" (127). Super Goat Man winds up not only another Lethem superhero who meets mixed success at superheroism but also another Lethem academic (like Philip Engstrand in *As She Climbed across the Table* or Cicero Lookins in *Dissident Gardens*) who is less than effectual, to put it kindly.

Lethem's next major book, *The Disappointment Artist* (2005), is the closest thing to traditional autobiography we have seen from this writer. Where the later collection *The Ecstasy of Influence* is largely comprised of critical essays that contain the occasional personal element, the reverse is true of *The Disappointment Artist.* These are personal essays that also happen to pay insightful tribute to artists and artworks about which Lethem is particularly passionate. He writes about his near-lifelong obsession with the John Ford western *The Searchers,* a vital intertext for Lethem's own *Girl in Landscape.* He offers an oddly touching remembrance of seeing *Star Wars* in the same theater twenty-one times in the summer of 1977. There is an account of Lethem's youthful discovery and wholesale surrender to the work of the sci-fi pioneer Philip K. Dick, including his completist quest to locate copies of all of Dick's out-of-print novels and his work in his twenties with the Philip K. Dick Society. The book's last essay, "The Beards," includes short sections devoted to the teenaged Lethem's affinities for Nicolas Roeg's *The Man Who Fell to Earth,* Pink Floyd's *Wish You Were Here,* and the late films of Jean-Luc Godard, among other artworks.

Near its conclusion is an image that had already appeared in earlier Lethem works and will play an important role in *Chronic City:* the living space packed full of books and music, which Lethem summarizes as "room as brain" (*TDA* 147). The image "began with the suspicion that I'd externalized my own brain, for anyone who cared to look. The simpler, and perhaps deeper, truth lies in the comparison more obvious to others: that the empires of data storage make up a castle or armor or hermit-crab's shell for my tender self" (147). Dylan Ebdus's wall of CDs; the quasi-archive of "The Vision"; the book-lined office of a physics professor in *As She Climbed across the Table,* compared to "a blown-up model of the interior of his skull" (78): all are images of people who live in a kind of symbiotic relationship with the reading and listening materials they love. So far Lethem has mostly emphasized the pleasures of such a mode of living. *Chronic City* will question its efficacy.

Lethem's first novel following *The Fortress of Solitude,* and the novel preceding *Chronic City,* is *You Don't Love Me Yet* (2007), a romantic comedy of sorts that is also a rather deliberately slight rock-and-roll novel. *You Don't Love Me Yet* received some of Lethem's harshest reviews, at least since *Motherless Brooklyn* and *The Fortress of Solitude* had announced his arrival as a major

American novelist. Many were put off by the novel's intentionally light tone and modest ambition, especially as it came on the heels of *The Fortress of Solitude,* Lethem's longest and most complex novel to that point.

Most intriguingly for the reader or critic interested in Lethem's aesthetic emphases on influence, appreciation, and appropriation, though, is the innovative way that Lethem approached the question of approved adaptation of *You Don't Love Me Yet.* Several Lethem novels have been optioned for feature film adaptation, though as yet none has become a completed production. A handful of Lethem's short stories have become short films, while "Light and the Sufferer," from *The Wall of the Sky, the Wall of the Eye,* became a feature released in 2007. Upon the publication of *You Don't Love Me Yet,* Lethem announced an open call for proposals for a feature adaptation of the novel, promising to select the strongest proposal and give away the film rights for free, in exchange for 2 percent of the completed film's budget should it receive a full distribution deal. Additionally, Lethem and the selected filmmaker would agree to release all adaptation rights for *You Don't Love Me Yet* into the public domain five years after the initial film's premiere, allowing other artists to create any other artworks using Lethem's novel as source material. In May 2007 Lethem selected the filmmaker Greg Marcks as the recipient of the initial film rights to *You Don't Love Me Yet.*[3]

As a companion piece to this arrangement, Lethem launched a Web site called the Promiscuous Materials Project, offering a handful of short stories, including four of the nine from *Men and Cartoons,* to any interested artists for use as freely available source material. Also offered for reuse were the lyrics, written by Lethem, attributed to the fictional band in *You Don't Love Me Yet.* The Promiscuous Materials Web site now also serves as a central location for links to recordings of those lyrics as well as information regarding short films based on Promiscuous Materials short fiction.

Chronic City is every bit as ambitious as *The Fortress of Solitude,* but its narrative scope is narrower: no decade-spanning panoramic breadth or cross-country trips. Instead nearly the entirety of the novel is set in Manhattan and follows only a handful of major characters. The narrator Chase Insteadman is a former child star, best known for his appearance on a perennially syndicated but rather silly sitcom called *Martyr & Pesty;* set for life as a result of residuals from his show's constant reruns, Chase has become a New York man-about-town, in demand as a party guest because of his natural charm and an unusual personal story in the news. His fiancée, Janice Trumbull, is trapped on an orbiting space station. Perkus Tooth is a general culture sponge who resists being called a rock critic and was once considered a major counterculture figure as a result of his trademark broadsheet publications. Chase's contact at

Criterion compares him to "Hunter Thompson meets Pauline Kael, for about five minutes" (*CC* 7). Perkus's old friend Richard Abneg now works in the New York City mayor's office as a fixer; also in Perkus's circle is Oona Laszlo, a professional ghostwriter who specializes in quickie memoirs by "traumatized athletes, frostbitten Everest climbers who have to wear plastic noses, etcetera" (44). Oona is an object of both Chase's and Perkus's desire.

To put it bluntly, Chase may well be Lethem's least astute protagonist. *Chronic City*'s New York is a befuddling place, shrouded in a mysterious gray fog and being inexplicably destroyed by a giant tiger. Chase knows of these oddities but thinks little of them. On seeing the new "WAR FREE EDITION" of the *New York Times,* his only thought is, "Ah yes. . . . You could opt out now" (*CC* 74). Chase has no more explanation of any of this than we do as the novel begins; indeed the book works in part because in Chase we find "as our apparent guide a narrator on par with our own cluelessness."[4] He has happily floated around the upper echelons of New York society for most of his adult life, Lethem reminds us, and he appears to have given little thought to why he lives as he does because, generally, he has never had to. Chase has perfected a persona that is blandly affable: "There's something pleasant about me," he modestly allows (28). Chase's inertia as the novel begins is considerable. He is at the Criterion office to record a voice-over for the bonus features of a DVD reissue, reading statements by a director whom he admits he has never heard of before. He confesses, "This was the only sort of stuff I did anymore, riding the exhaust of my former and vanishing celebrity" (2). He no longer acts professionally, "unless you'd call my every waking moment a kind of performance" (64).

To his benefit and his chagrin, Perkus recognizes this on his first meeting with Chase. He confronts Chase over dinner at Jackson Hole, Perkus's old-school diner of choice, and says, "So, you've gotten to this point by being cute, haven't you, Chase?" (*CC* 10). Perkus has him pegged: "You haven't changed, you're like a dreamy child, that's the secret of your appeal" (11). Later, when a waitress at Jackson Hole garbles Chase's name, turning him into "Chase Unperson," Perkus explodes in "bitter hilarity" (182). Perkus's forthrightness catches Chase off guard, but Chase also knows that Perkus is right. They become fast friends.

For a while *Chronic City* is a rollicking, funny hang-out novel. Chase points out that "very soon after our first encounter I'd come to adore and need Perkus" (*CC* 6), and they spend hours on end together. Much of that time is comprised of Perkus's (overdue, in his view) aesthetic education of Chase, as he recommends books, movies, and music as "essential viewings" to his new friend (17). Perkus's attitude mixes boundless excitement at introducing Chase to new things with utter exasperation at all the art and entertainment that Chase does not already know. These listening and viewing sessions, fueled by marijuana and Jackson Hole burgers, turn "Perkus's apartment [into] a place for consuming archival wonders," Chase narrates, sharing Perkus's passion for unheralded cultural artifacts such as "bootlegged unreleased recordings by those in Tooth's musical pantheon, like Chet Baker, Nina Simone, or Neil Young, and grainy tapes of scarce film noir taped off late-night television broadcasts" (17–18). In Chase's first conversations with him at Jackson Hole, Perkus holds forth on Monte Hellman, Griel Marcus, "the genius of *The Gnuppet Show*," Slavoj Žižek, Norman Mailer, and Alfred Hitchcock (12). Perkus even screens an old episode of *Columbo* in which the young Chase Insteadman appeared, providing for Chase an exegesis of "details I could never have bothered to observe, either then, as a child actor on the set, or as a viewer now" (19). Even as Chase clearly plays student to Perkus the teacher, the friendship is touchingly genuine. It also revels in the ecstasy of influence, passionate enjoyment of one's favorite art, every bit as much as Dylan and Mingus do trading comic books or blaring funk records in *The Fortress of Solitude.*

For all its ecstasy of influence, *Chronic City* also contains Lethem's most direct invocation of the anxiety of influence in Bloomian terms. At the center of this novel lies Perkus Tooth's fascination with chaldrons, large, perfectly shaped vases. Perkus and his friends become so taken with viewing photographs of chaldrons that the need to possess one becomes all-encompassing, superseding all other desires. For readers well versed in American fiction from around the turn of the twenty-first century, this premise invokes a central plot strand in another novel that serves as a key influence on and intertext for Lethem's work: David Foster Wallace's *Infinite Jest* (1996). Wallace's masterwork includes an experimental film, the title "entertainment," that is said to be so engrossing that anyone who views it is literally amused to death. Viewers find themselves so entertained that even the life-sustaining urges to eat and sleep get fully neutralized to the point of paralysis.

Lethem introduces a clear Wallace analogue early in *Chronic City* by depicting Perkus's ownership of a mammoth novel by the (also three-named but fictional) author Ralph Warden Meeker called *Obstinate Dust*. Like *Infinite Jest, Obstinate Dust* is a book with more owners than readers, more starters than finishers. It is worth noting that unlike *Infinite Jest, Obstinate Dust* seems rather bad. *Obstinate Dust* is entirely italicized (*CC* 101–2); perhaps Lethem emphasizes typography as a tongue-in-cheek reference to the hundreds of fine-print endnotes in Wallace's novel. *Obstinate Dust* enters Lethem's plot when Oona and Chase visit *Urban Fjord,* an art installation in Manhattan by Laird Noteless that is essentially a deep chasm built directly into the earth. Noteless, for whom Oona is ghostwriting a memoir, creates lavish but controversial earthworks projects. Chase has just bought a copy of *Obstinate Dust* from an on-street book peddler who also happens to be an acquaintance of Perkus, and when some bystanders at the abyss explain that it has become customary to throw something into the hole, Oona persuades Chase to toss in his copy of Meeker's novel. First, Chase thinks, "I had to tell myself it wasn't Perkus Tooth I'd be symbolically interring in that pit, but Ralph Warden Meeker" (111). At any rate, he figures that "it would be a relief to walk the return path without the asymmetrical sink-weight in my pocket" (111). He watches the book fall into the gorge, but it is too deep for Chase to see the book land.

What better way for Lethem to reject thoroughly the anxiety of influence than to have his protagonist buy a copy of (something clearly quite analogous to) the book to which his own novel might be reasonably compared, only to have said protagonist then throw that book into an actual abyss. On top of that, Chase claims a physical relief, a weight he no longer carries. Lethem explains in this gesture that while *Chronic City* might share some conceptual overlap with *Infinite Jest,* any direct comparison between the two novels should not be taken too far. This is not that kind of book, he is telling us, so go peddle your pseudo-Oedipal metaphorical interpretation elsewhere. Lethem has said that he considered removing the Meeker book and all scenes including it, since Wallace committed suicide while Lethem was completing *Chronic City.* Instead he realized that to edit Meeker out would be "as though I'd be erasing [Wallace] in some way. . . . I put it in again at the end of the book to make it mean a little more, and then I felt that it would be okay" (*Conv* 173). *Obstinate Dust* will reenter Lethem's characters' ken later in the novel, but only after chaldrons have been so thoroughly demystified and redefined that no direct comparison of the quasi-magical vases to Wallace's deadly film seems plausible anymore. Oona accidentally buys for Perkus, instead of Meeker's *Obstinate Dust,* a slim volume of minimalist poetry called *Immaculate Rust.* It is as if to say that influences can never fully be tossed into the void. Lethem hastens to add that the Wallace reference should be taken as tribute, not critique; or in other words, it should reflect the ecstasy of influence, not the anxiety of influence. "I don't really bother putting in anything [in my work] that I dislike," Lethem explains. "So people are often thinking I'm attacking stuff that I'm actually terrifically interested in. It's just that in conversation they sometimes get some scuff marks on them" (*Conv* 174).

Lethem's Wallace analogue, Meeker, is far from the only famous figure in *Chronic City* who has some real-world equivalent. *Chronic City* blurs the lines between fiction and reality effectively via Lethem's use of fictional celebrity characters, some of whom are clearly meant to be comparable to real famous figures while others have no clear real-world equal. Manhattan arts commissioner Russ Grinspoon, a sometime actor with a "frizzy reddish halo of hair" and who is the higher-voiced half of a once-popular musical duo, bears a close resemblance to Art Garfunkel (*CC* 264, 269). Sandra Saunders Eppling, introduced as an advocate on behalf of a wild bird who has taken up residence outside an apartment building, is also, we learn, a onetime Elvis Presley costar and a three-named former sitcom mom (51–52). For readers familiar with the avian Fifth Avenue resident Pale Male (and his celebrity advocates), it is clear: Sandra Saunders Eppling equals Mary Tyler Moore. Florian Ib, who Perkus says worked on "*The Gnuppet Movie*" (86)—one wonders if Lethem foresaw potential legal troubles in using the term "Muppet" directly, as the trademark is now owned by the famously litigious Walt Disney Company—but whom Perkus later dismisses as a hack, refers to director-Muppeteer Frank Oz. A few pages later Chase meets Oona at the funeral of one Emil Junrow, a popular science writer (55–57). The title of Junrow's well-known book *I Can't Quite Believe You Said That, Dr. Junrow* is a dead giveaway, making it clear that he parallels *Surely You're Joking, Mr. Feynman*'s author, Richard Feynman. Lethem's Feynmanesque Junrow also includes a dash of Carl Sagan, though, as "a relentless proselytizer for the peaceful exploration of space" (56), making it clear that Lethem's pseudocelebs are not one-to-one analogues. *Chronic City* is no roman à clef. The earthworks artist Laird Noteless, for instance, creator of art projects such as "*Local Chasm, Demapped Intersection, Former Landmark,* [and] *Erased Atrocity*" in addition to *Urban Fjord* (207), resembles Christo, creator of, among others, the 2005 Central Park installation *The Gates*. Where Christo seeks to remake the world, though, Noteless's chasms and erasures suggest a desire to destroy the world entirely. Then there is Morrison Groom, the maverick film director and onetime Brando collaborator whom Perkus idolizes: as central as he is to Perkus's aesthetic, he has no real-life analogue.

Of course many readers and critics have wondered where Perkus Tooth fits on this spectrum: is he more a Morrison Groom or a Russ Grinspoon? In truth, he appears to lie between the two. Rivka Galchen posits that Perkus Tooth's partial inspiration is the rock critic Paul Nelson, whom Lethem knew and has acknowledged as an inspiration for Perkus on a few occasions.[5] On other occasions, though, Lethem is comically cagey about just who Perkus might be. In a short 2005 piece for the *Washington Post*, Lethem claimed that "Perkus Tooth wouldn't exist without the precedent of the character Rudolph Menthol, from Rufus Firefly's great novel *Years between Islands*."[6] The gag here is that no such novel exists. Rufus Firefly is Groucho Marx's character in *Duck Soup*, while *Years between Islands* sounds rather akin to *Days between Stations*, a 1985 novel by Steve Erickson. It should come as no surprise that Steve Erickson, an avowed influence on Lethem (*Conv* 52, 54), shares Lethem's interest in straddling the boundaries between the fabulism of sci-fi and more traditionally defined literary fiction.

Speaking of fabulism, there is a mysterious, giant, possibly mechanical tiger destroying New York in this novel. Chase hears Perkus's homeless friend Biller speak quite matter-of-factly of this animal and the destruction in its wake early in the text, though at first he does not entirely credit Biller: "A tiger could be a homeless man's emblem, I thought, of all the terrors that pursued him" (*CC* 22). He gives more credence to a discussion of it between Richard and Perkus, though, who explains that the tiger demolished "one of the city's primary water mains last week" (55). Soon thereafter, we learn, it has "razed a twenty-four-hour Korean market on 103rd Street" (74), and Richard now serves on an ad hoc government committee about the tiger, complete with its own active internal listserv of tiger-based discussion (133). Eventually Richard will explain that the tiger is a "machine, a robot, that's right, for digging a subway tunnel" (162). He compares this tiger to the pair of digging machines used to build the Chunnel under the English Channel, connecting England and France. Those two digging machines met in the middle, under the channel, and were then buried away from the tunnel itself. New York is using its machine to build a new subway line, but, he suspects, being the sole machine devoted to the purpose, "the thing got lonely. . . . At night sometimes it comes up from underneath and sort of, you know, ravages around" (163). The city is loath to stop it because of the demand for a Second Avenue line, nor have they sought to correct any eyewitness who has attributed the destruction to an escaped tiger. Shortly the tiger will take down Jackson Hole and with it much of the block that includes Perkus's building (237).

One more important slippage between reality and its ambiguously defined opposite in *Chronic City* concerns Perkus's enthusiastic admiration for Marlon Brando. Perkus refuses to believe Richard's off-the-cuff comment that Brando has recently died. His skepticism is more than just a fan's denial, however, as the suggestions pile up that Brando's death might be every bit as much a hoax as the giant tiger is. For Perkus, Brando represents "the living avatar of the unexpressed, a human enunciation of the remaining hopes for our murdered era" (*CC* 85). Brando's greatest moment, for Perkus, came "when he sent Sacheen Littlefeather to accept the Oscar [for *The Godfather*] in his place," as "it's the most amazing conflation of the American Imaginary" in that it links protest against American genocide of Native Americans (and its glorification on film) to the story of Don Corleone, an immigrant who does "the American dream, capitalism, I mean, more ruthlessly than the founding fathers could have ever dreaded" (85). Perkus's overheated explanation reveals the position of the underappreciated critic at its most aggressive. He starts with a familiar artistic subject but recenters it so that the piece of it that once seemed most marginal (the Oscar refusal speech, not the Oscar-winning performance) is now most important. In addition there is a veiled hostility in the claim that Perkus, and only Perkus, really has the key to understanding this thing that not everyone else gets at all. After Perkus doubts the news of Brando's demise, Richard pulls up Brando's Wikipedia page on Perkus's ancient computer to show him the paragraph about Brando's July 2004 death. On another visit to Wikipedia a few pages later—in a scene that, significantly, occurs after Richard has revealed the truth about the tiger—that paragraph has been replaced by a discussion of "rumors of Brando's death" and a notice that "the truthfulness of this article has been questioned. It is believed that some or all of its contents may constitute a hoax" (167). Chase will reveal in the novel's final pages that online arguments continue over whether Brando is alive or not (464–65). After Richard has let the tiger out of the bag, so to speak, slippages between reality and something that is not reality continue to grow.

Brian McHale argues that in postmodern fiction and sci-fi alike, the core questions characters must answer are less epistemological than ontological. He explains that "typical postmodernist questions bear either on the ontology of the literary text itself or on the ontology of the world which it projects, for instance: . . . What happens when different kinds of world are placed in confrontation, or when boundaries between worlds are violated?"[7] To apply this idea to *Chronic City,* a novel deeply interested in the implications of multiple existent worlds, Chase's real conundrum lies not in finding any single piece of information that will help him make sense of the world but in figuring out what kind of world he actually lives in—one with or without a mechanical tiger, one in which Brando can only be either dead or alive.

Perkus idolizes Brando because he understands him to represent all the untapped artistic power that can possibly exist in a time that, in his view, now values wealth over creativity. As he tells Chase, "Brando's a figure of freedom, just as much as that chaldron we just saw" (*CC* 155). If Brando is the dominant symbol of *Chronic City* for the novel's first eighty pages or so, it will soon be supplanted by the symbology of the potent chaldron. Perkus first sees a chaldron at the office of Strabo Blandiana, an acupuncturist to whom he has been referred by Chase. On his first visit, he vaguely registers "a silver-framed photograph, of an enigmatic orange-glowing ceramic vase against a blank white backdrop" (77). On his second visit, seeing the chaldron photo is a far more intense aesthetic experience, apparently putting him in touch with the transcendent. "The vase was lit," Perkus notices, "to throw no shadow against either wall or table . . . the vase seemed to have its own message for Perkus: Have you neglected Beauty? . . . The vase sheltered Perkus like a kindly cove . . . [it] spoke to Perkus, simply, of not the possibility but the fact of another world" (89–90). He first hears the term "chaldron" from Strabo, who identifies the photograph simply as a "gift from another patient" (91). Now possessing a word to attach to the image, Perkus instantly decides he must own one.

Perkus starts looking for chaldrons on eBay, a dicey proposition given his old computer and dial-up Internet access, and finds some for sale, "advertised with photographs much like that he'd seen on Strabo's wall" (*CC* 92). Perkus's aesthetic education of Chase, and with it the loose, slacker-y vibe of their visits together, gets fully replaced by what Chase will come to call "his unhealthy onanistic chaldron hunt" (117). At the height of Perkus's desire, Chase is concerned that Perkus's yen for chaldrons has tamped down the critical zeal that once seemed Perkus's very life force: "I would have given anything to hear him talking about Brando or Mailer" instead, he comments (181). Still, chaldrons are in demand evidently; when the frenzied online bidding drives them out of Perkus's price range, Richard steps in with his own credit card. At one point a chaldron sells on eBay for fourteen thousand dollars; later, forty grand even (149, 161). Meanwhile, Perkus and Chase's few other close friends are drawn in to chaldron mania as well. Chase grants the chaldron power that is both binding and destructive, as it has the ability to destroy "all available frames or contexts, gently burning itself through our retinas to hover in our collective mind's eye, a beholding that transcended optics" (141). Richard's girlfriend Georgina calls the chaldron "a kind of door," making Chase reflect that "its effect was to make constructed things, theories and arguments, cities and hairstyles, attitudes, sentences, all seem tawdry, impoverished, lame" (142). Significantly, particularly in light of what we will later learn about chaldrons, Chase posits the chaldron and its world as hyperreal, as more real than any world Chase could already know. Eventually, Perkus will decide that the delirium of bidding for chaldrons has replaced his desire actually to own one. He tells Chase that the ritual of music, bidding, and marijuana "is enough. It gets me through, knowing that it's out there" (145). While Perkus suggests that bidding alone is an aesthetic, near-transcendent experience for him, it is also not hard to interpret this as the losing bidder's expression of sour grapes. But by then Perkus's entire circle has developed a chaldron obsession. Chase is pretty sure he sees a chaldron-shaped balloon in the Macy's Thanksgiving parade (202).

Perkus's chaldron-free peace gets challenged four chapters later. All of the main characters are attending a ritzy holiday party thrown by New York City mayor Jules Arnheim amid a massive blizzard. When arts commissioner / Garfunkel analogue Russ Grinspoon invites Chase and Perkus upstairs to see "a certain rare vase in Arnheim's collection" (*CC* 271), readers can safely assume that it is a chaldron. Perkus and Chase see the mayor's chaldron but cannot reach it, as it is encased in a vitrine and nestled into a high nook near a skylight. Though Chase will leave, Perkus will wind up spending the night on the staircase, enraptured by the chaldron, and he will be found in the morning by Claire Carter, another mayor's aide, whom Richard has already characterized as tough as nails.

To Perkus (and to the reader) Claire reveals information about chaldrons that both disappoints and frees him. Lethem introduces the fictional Yet Another World, a vast and game-like cyberspace simulation of reality akin to Second Life, when Perkus's once-homeless friend Biller, who now lives in a "weird new apartment . . . with forty or fifty dogs," explains the unlikely source of his newfound wealth (*CC* 223). Biller has been manufacturing virtual treasure inside Yet Another World and selling it for real money (224–26). Claire now explains the genesis of Yet Another World and the vital role that chaldrons play within its social organization and economy. Claire's brother Linus, a computer whiz and virtual-reality designer, created chaldrons as an element of Yet Another World, for which Claire helped Linus secure financing (327). The levels of nested realities here are considerable and get comically ungainly: Lethem's novel includes a fictional cyberspace alternate reality that has a real-world analogue in a cyberspace alternate reality that actually exists. Yet Another World has developed its own alternate currency, meaning that its participants can be wealthy people within this other world. Linus had created chaldrons as a "scattered few objets d'art" within this rich cyberlandscape, though their rarity, unlike manufactured treasure such as Biller's, had begun to bring out "acquisitive frenzy" in some players such that "the chaldron quickly became the supreme symbol of the game's elite" (331). Chaldrons become valuable in Yet Another World not solely for their beauty but also for their scarcity, and unlike anything else in this digital universe, they cannot be successfully duplicated. Linus, genius programmer that he is, has created "a few expert subroutines for rooting out and destroying any counterfeits put into circulation" (331). Chaldrons, "fundamentally imaginary though they might be, had begun had begun trading in the 'real' world for hundreds then thousands of dollars," Perkus learns (331). In appreciation for her help in getting Yet Another World off the ground, Linus has given Claire ten chaldrons. She is uninterested in virtual life, though she has realized that soon she will "be able to put future kids through college on the things" (332). The mayor's chaldron, a gift from Claire, is a hologram, to Perkus's considerable disappointment (328).

All the while Perkus had been bidding on eBay for virtual objects, never actual vases. The art objects that had never existed have become primarily a commodity. The world that Linus has created, which once bore the possibility of being a better world than reality, winds up as socially stratified as the real world. Oddly enough, *Chronic City* has become in certain regards a book more about wealth than about art, as comparable to Don DeLillo's New York–set novel of cybercapital *Cosmopolis* (2003) as to anything else. Ecstatic appreciation has failed Perkus, and since that mode of living has been central to his identity as a critic, he must now find another way to live.

Before explaining how Perkus's new life works as a depiction of the limits of the ecstasy of influence's usefulness, if not a rejection of it, it is worth establishing what kind of critic Perkus really has been. Susan Eldred, Perkus and Chase's shared contact at Criterion, calls him "quite an amazing critic. When I was at NYU all my friends and I used to idolize him" (*CC* 7). Perkus takes pains to point out whenever possible, however, that even though he sometimes writes about pop music, he is *not* a rock critic. He calls rock critics "super-high-functioning autistics" who "gather for purposes of mutual consolation" (14, 15). "They believe they're *experts,*" he hisses (15), and in his most self-loathing moments, the adult Dylan Ebdus would agree. Perkus once had the opportunity to write a book, "a compilation of the broadsides," but it went nowhere because his editor "saw [Perkus] as a rock critic" (47).

Lethem rarely depicts Perkus at work, but when he does, Perkus comes to life essentially as a creative appropriator and collage artist, working in a manner comparable to Lethem himself in "The Ecstasy of Influence." Chase describes Perkus's work space at home as "a mad tatter of clippings, books with spines pressed open by whatever lay to hand . . . and with their pages mutilated, paragraphs excised and stickily transferred to gigantic cardboard backings, collaged into wild conjunctions, like vast scholarly punk-rock liner notes" (*CC* 82). This vision of the critic casts Perkus as a remixer, a sampler, and quite possibly an artist, as Lethem has effectively blurred the lines here that separate the critic from the creator, given how central appropriation has become to postmodern artistic practice. Perkus holds in his hands strips of text he has carved from these books: one compares the Beatles to the Beats; the second compares the Beatles to Bret Easton Ellis; and a third reads like a bit of Foucaultesque social theory (84). It remains unclear how Perkus intended to use these, but Lethem makes clear that he has borrowed more material than he has created from scratch.

Lethem is as much an appropriation artist as Perkus; *Chronic City*'s final page is a list of Lethem's borrowings, making clear that the first and third of the fragments Perkus holds are from real texts, meaning that the second, oddly, is not. Additionally, Lethem clarifies that certain phrases and sentences in *Chronic City* originate in works by notable writers such as James Baldwin, Seymour Krim, and Saul Bellow. Indeed, for a book so full of artist figures of one sort or another (actors, writers, critics, earthworks creators, and software designers), artistic originality is hardly mentioned in *Chronic City*. Presumably Lethem has so dispensed with the idea of originality as valuable (or even possible) in "The Ecstasy of Influence" that it seems a nonissue now. In fact the only artist who goes to bat for the idea of authenticity in art—Laird Noteless, getting punchy with Perkus as he snarls, "I don't work in pixels . . . I work in stone and soil" (*CC* 268)—winds up cast as a bit of a crank for doing so.

Perkus, however, like every other artist who was once ahead of his time, finds that the times have caught up to him. Lethem casts Perkus's single attempt in the novel to paste up broadsides, as he did in the old days, as a dreadful failure. His photocopied work bears "none of the grandeur of his famous broadsides," Chase notes, and since the central image of the flyer is a photo of a polar bear adrift on a floating piece of ice, the finished work resembles nothing more than "a 'lost dog' flyer" (*CC* 221, 222). Chase likens the "scraps of visual noise" to "gum wrappers" (222). Later, Oona will suggest that trying to blend the roles of artist and critic is no longer a winning proposition, as she explains that actually doing research for a book on Laird Noteless resulted in its rejection from her publisher (372). So if originality is hardly open to artists anymore and Perkus's old creative form now seems hopelessly uncreative and originality was hardly ever open to critics in this novel's world, then what is a character such as Perkus left to do? The answer: reframe the work of the critic as that of the curator.

An oddity of the semantics of early twenty-first-century pop criticism is the sudden and visible upswing in use of the term "curator." Lethem introduces this idea and this language in *Chronic City* as early as possible: on the first page of the book, Chase refers to the "curatorial geniuses at Criterion" (*CC* 1). In *Retromania,* a book that suggests that originality in pop music in particular has been hamstrung by years of reverence for past styles, the excellent (sorry, Perkus) rock critic Simon Reynolds writes, "I first noticed the buzz-phrase 'curated by' at some point in the early 2000s, when it started to infiltrate the left-field fringes of music. . . . Activities that once would have been humbly described as selecting a compilation or booking bands for a festival now came coated in the high-falutin' gloss of curation."[8] He continues, in a chapter wittily titled "Good Citations," "The aspirational use of the word 'curating' by musicians suggested that the same skill set required to run an art gallery or organise a museum exhibition was being applied to the formation of a band's sonic identity."[9] This line of thought can be transplanted easily from the musical world to the literary world, and Lethem is hardly immune. In addition to editing multiple volumes of Philip K. Dick novels and the large published excerpt of Dick's journals, Lethem has written more than a handful of introductions to reprints of older novels. Asked about this work, Lethem explains, "I see this work as a curatorial impulse, the same one that used to be expressed for me by my work in an antiquarian bookstore, where I'd cultivate and groom the literature section" (*Conv* 98). Indeed late in *Fear of Music,* Lethem will compare David Byrne, running circles around the stage at the end of "Life during Wartime" in the Talking Heads concert film *Stop Making Sense,* to "a proud curator racing through the rooms of his museum gesturing at the wonders in his collection" (*FoM* 122). The description could also apply to the manic Perkus Tooth (who, granted, would probably not break into a full run) or to Lethem himself at his most curatorial. In describing musicians who appear at first glance overly reverential of the past, Reynolds writes that such a move is not about "showing off or connoisseurial conceit; it's more about paying tribute, about ancestor worship."[10] To apply the concept to literature, Lethem's appropriation works as literary filial piety, particularly in elements such as *Chronic City*'s encoded nods to David Foster Wallace.

A lifetime's collection can become a solipsistic monument to one's own consumption (like the wall of fourteen hundred CDs in front of which Dylan and Abby lock horns as part 3 of *The Fortress of Solitude* opens), or it can turn one's own home—and by extension one's own psyche—into a museumlike archive: impeccably managed but preserved without the artworks' use value in mind. At least Perkus's personal archive appears to be constantly in use. Instead of seeing pristine organization on his first visit, Chase explains, "books filled the open cabinet spaces above the sink. The countertop was occupied with a CD player and hundreds of disks" (*CC* 9). Seeing Perkus's vintage dinette set, he registers Perkus as "nothing if not a collector" (9). Contrast that with Oona's place: "The minimal shelves stood free, and were loaded with books sporadically bunched in spine-wrecking slouches, or laid sideways to begin with" (206). Of the two, Perkus is the curator, owning more media than any shelves could ever corral. He also wields the skill of turning his opinions into facts in the minds of those who listen. Chase tries to imagine "what it would take for me to burnish my favorites into myth like Perkus had done" (242). The implication is that he cannot.

Later in the novel, Perkus is torn from his personal archive when the mechanical tiger destroys his street, and chaldrons have been revealed to him to be fake. Lethem tells us that since Perkus had for so long functioned "from a platform of cultural clues arranged into jigsaw sense, [he] had gone years certain his solipsism was a pretty good home" (*CC* 341). Yet the loss of everything he knows and values forces him to find a new mode of operation. "Perkus had let go of things more dear that apartments," Lethem narrates. "His encounter with the mayor's chaldron spared him such simplicities: an apartment was only a container for bodies, after all, while a chaldron was a container for what under duress he'd call souls" (*CC* 322). The implication is that the apartment was just a living space whose loss he will weather, but the loss of the possibility of transcendence through chaldrons may be too much for him.

It is important to note that Lethem does not posit Perkus's solipsism and loneliness as the inevitable lot of the collector or the cultural enthusiast. Chase describes Susan Eldred, his contact at Criterion, as "what a sane, female version of Perkus Tooth might resemble: you didn't have to be mad to care for mad stuff" (*CC* 198). But Chase had been coming to realize for a while that Perkus's frequent claims to be anything but a rock critic were a defense mechanism. After Perkus takes such delight in Chase being referred to as "Chase Unperson," Chase begins viewing his friend "as a creature formed of anger," or at least schadenfreude (*CC* 183). In addition Perkus's certainty that "the mayor's astounding chaldron had no appreciator besides himself" (*CC* 323) sounds quite a bit like those Stan Brakhage experts in *The Fortress of Solitude* who were aggressively certain that they were the best viewers possible of their idol's films. Rock critics, in Perkus's view, "are like little animals that live in holes" and constantly want Perkus to join them in their "pledge of allegiance of the Elite Despised" (*CC* 262, 333). Perkus articulates the latter thought after meeting Claire Carter and recognizing her as a member, like most rock critics, of "the we-nerds-run-the-universe school" (*CC* 333). Lethem has articulated what he calls "the self-willed exile of the minority population" in discussing why so many sci-fi fans want little to do with literary culture on a larger scale, but his description easily applies to Perkus as well. Lethem explains, "Outsider identity becomes defiant—the brand of the outcast worn as a badge of subcultural credibility. Which therefore propagates the problem from within the outcast community as well. . . . Anytime people define themselves by the outlines of their own rejection, it's made easy to go on rejecting them" (*Conv* 113). Having so internalized the role he has established for himself as a self-proclaimed and underrecognized genius, having been so convinced that his taste in most everything will always be the best taste in the room, and having clearly seen that approach to the world fail, Perkus must now find a new role.

Figuring that he has nowhere else to go, Perkus goes to the Friendreth Canine Apartments. This strange living space gets introduced, well before Perkus goes there, as the creation of a widowed heiress who insisted that abandoned domesticated animals "need to inhabit human surroundings . . . dogs should live in homes, not cages" (*CC* 136). As a fixer in the mayor's office, Richard "had to fend off advocates for the homeless, who'd claimed Friendreth's dogs lived better than some of Manhattan's humans" (136). Those advocates, Lethem makes clear, were correct. Perkus takes up residence with Ava, a three-legged pit bull, in a fairly well-furnished and roomy living space. Temporarily pulling away from Chase into an even more spartan existence, Perkus has made himself half of a new dynamic duo. "Those first days were all sensual intimacy, a feast of familiarization, an orgy of, yes, pair-bonding" as Perkus gets to know Ava (315). In communing with this abandoned dog instead of photos of chaldrons or thoughts of Marlon Brando films, Perkus finds "a new doctrine: recover bodily absolutes, journey into the real" (318). Furthermore, Perkus's newfound desire for the real leads him to put critical activity aside: "He held off interpretation for now . . . interpretation could wait" (318). That said, he does not entirely give up enjoyment of popular culture. Instead he latches more closely than ever before onto a smaller number of artifacts.

After years of curating an enormous personal archive, Perkus winds up taking in whatever books or music he finds in other dog apartments. As a result he develops some unlikely artistic attachments. He gets obsessed with the Steve Martin pastiche movie *Dead Men Don't Wear Plaid,* partly because it is a curatorial movie (*CC* 391), a 1982 comedy that incorporates clips from classic noir films. Perkus's love for it suggests that the curatorial impulse in him has not left entirely. Chase suggests that Perkus saw himself as like the Martin character "for the way he breezed in and out of the archival footage, reanimating his own pantheon of heroes. This was analogous to how Perkus saw himself moving amid Brando, Groom, Krim, Cassavetes, Mailer, Marplot, Serling, and all the others" (391). In the desultory artworks he finds in the Friendreth Apartments, though, Perkus rediscovers the use value of art as opposed to its status or collector value.

Like Dylan Ebdus's musical loves, Perkus Tooth's songs of choice bear huge symbolic meaning, particularly in light of how he has forsaken his vast archive of books and music in favor of only that pop material that seems essential and life-giving. One record "now stood in for all he'd ever known or lost or cared for" (*CC* 352). In another dog's apartment Perkus has found a copy of the 1978 New York–centric album *Some Girls* by the Rolling Stones, and he loves dancing with Ava to the record's closing track, "Shattered" (351–53). *Some Girls* has figured in *Chronic City* before, as Perkus uses its disco tune "Miss You" to help the group come back down to earth after a binge of eBay bidding on chaldrons. As Chase describes it, that song works because it brings them from the transcendent high of chaldron-mania back to lower, baser, carnal desires. Its evocation of late 1970s decadence makes Chase think of "stuff to make us grateful the chaldron hadn't translated us out of our discrete and horny bodies just yet" (151). Chase rejects the transcendent there, but he does imagine that the song has inspired connection between humans. Perkus revels in "Shattered" for its romantic vision of a depraved New York in ruins, but if it is bringing him connection with anyone, it is Ava the dog and not any human. Perkus's last musical love mentioned by name is the Warren Zevon song "Roland the Headless Thompson Gunner" (391), the last song that the terminally ill Zevon performed before his death in 2002. There Lethem does some supersubtle foreshadowing for pop fiends only.

For all of the joy that Perkus takes in his cultural loves even in the Friendreth Apartments, though, the solipsism is still there, leaving him profoundly isolated. Late in the novel, Perkus's failing health leads Chase and Richard to take him to a doctor. When they show up at Perkus's (and Ava's) apartment, they find Perkus with "*Immaculate Rust* in scissored remnants all around him, shattered like everything else that met Perkus's interested eye" (*CC* 399). While Chase would once have taken this as a positive sign—Perkus is working again—he now sees things more clearly. Yes, Perkus is remixing another artwork he likes (or in this case, one that he has on hand, more accurately), but he is doing it badly. Chase notes that now "the final destination" of his remixing is "the ransom note," as Perkus has been "kidnapped by his own theories" (399). Perkus insists on being taken to Strabo the acupuncturist, who immediately diagnoses Perkus with internal bleeding and recommends that they take Perkus straight to the emergency room.

For Perkus, to live is to interpret. The critical impulse is his life force. Having given up interpretation while living with Ava, now Perkus starts interpreting an infomercial in the hospital waiting room: "You could stage it off Broadway, it would be like Beckett, Chase, the most astounding avant-garde spectacle" (*CC* 412). While waiting with Perkus for a doctor, Chase muses that "the size of his loneliness was hard to contemplate. I suppose his kind of radical openness required barricades in some areas—he couldn't have let women pass easily through him and still make room for all those arcane references, all those wild conjectures, all those drugs, all that cosmic radiation flooding his brain. He'd shut the door to sex and in came chaldrons and Ava and hiccups instead" (416). Meanwhile, Perkus finally admits that he is a rock critic, calling his fellow rock critics "my brothers" (414). Chase is "startled" in this scene at Perkus's command to write Chase's name down on the hospital paperwork that gives him power of attorney should Perkus be unable to make decisions for himself (410). Perkus and Chase seem equally surprised in that moment by how close they have become. It is a tender moment given even more weight by Perkus's death in the hospital that night.

Motherless Brooklyn introduced a recurring feature in Lethem's fiction: relationships between two male characters that occasionally blur the lines between the homosocial and the homoerotic. Lionel goes through a phase in which one Tourette's tic manifests as a yen for kissing his male coworkers (*MB*

45). Later he will note, "Like a lover, I loved to make Minna laugh" (*MB* 66). That which is largely metaphorical and homosocial in *Motherless Brooklyn* becomes more literal and homoerotic in *The Fortress of Solitude,* given a few scenes in which Mingus and Dylan discuss adolescent sexual fantasies and eventually do some experimentation with each other. *Chronic City,* though, lacks this element altogether; for all of Janice's pining for Chase, Chase's on-again-off-again romance with Oona, and the relationship between Richard and Georgina, it is the least sexual of the major Lethem novels. Perkus views not just monogamy but any romantic coupling at all as hopelessly prosaic: "I always used to feel critical of anyone who fell into pair-bonding, like they were failing the test of reimagining all the basic premises" (*CC* 219). Perkus does speak of this in the past tense, as a take on the world that he has now rejected. That said, he does not apply the idea to himself, and he changes the subject soon thereafter. When Perkus admits to Chase, only hours before Perkus's death in the hospital, that he has never really had an adult relationship with a woman (*CC* 415), it becomes clear to Perkus that he has walled himself off from more experiences than he will ever realize. As Lethem has put it, enjoyment of any art can put its audience into a more intense relationship with reality, or it can make one turn "to hermetic isolation, to empty compromise, to retreat from community instead of an approach" (*Conv* 75). In that moment Lethem is referring to the adult Dylan Ebdus, but his description may fit Perkus Tooth's dilemma even more aptly.

Chronic City may appear at times a largely escapist fiction, given its touches of the fantastic, but, like *The Fortress of Solitude,* it emerges as an inescapably political novel, meditating as it often does on wealth, status, and public tragedy. Chase understands his level of privilege even as he affects an air of bohemian detachment: "Though I do dwell among the money people, that's incidental to what I like about the Upper East Side" (*CC* 65). Chase shares his name, after all, with the largest bank in America, one headquartered in Manhattan, no less. Lethem is hardly the first writer to depict New York as a kind of synecdoche for the entire nation; in *Chronic City* specifically, though, New York is greedy, decadent, and soulless. The prime examples of such in this novel are Rossmore and Arjuna Danzig, a wealthy, old-money couple who win a dinner date with Chase in a charity auction for the price of fifty thousand dollars (176). Chase arrives at their chosen restaurant to find that the Danzigs have paid to have the entire restaurant to themselves, and Rossmore proceeds to order Chase a "zillion-dollar frittata" that contains a whole lobster and an obscene amount of caviar (189, 192). We will find out much later from Claire Carter that it was Rossmore Danzig who funded Yet Another World. That patronage places

Rossmore at the unlikely center of the entire novel, since his money winds up enabling the existence of chaldrons and catalyzing one of the novel's major slippages between reality and virtuality.

Some of this novel's view of contemporary New York comes out of a nostalgia for a pre-1990s Manhattan that, in the retrospective views of many, made up for its higher crime rate with its lower cost of living and general vibrancy. Perkus sums this up in his first bull session with Chase, decrying "the ruination Giuliani's administration had brought to the sacred squalor of Times Square" (*CC* 12). Richard Abneg, we are told, "had begun as a radical, an anarchist. His formative event [was] the Tompkins Square Park riots. . . . Now, ultimate irony, Abneg worked for Mayor Arnheim, managing the undoing of rent stabilization" (32). That said, Richard still hates Claire Carter, viewing her as "the symbol of the destruction of the city's soul" (333). Meanwhile, Perkus has come to think of the city as a shadow of its former self. At first this happens because of his obsession with chaldrons, whose resplendent reality can only make Manhattan "seem an enactment" (152). Later, Perkus becomes convinced that "there was some rupture in this city . . . we've been living in a place that's a replica of itself, a fragile simulacrum. . . . A theme park, really!" (389). Given the ubiquity of the metaphor of "Disneyfication" in recent discussions of American urban renewal, Perkus's claim may not be far off the mark. Still, Perkus can get nostalgic too, and he can inculcate that nostalgia in others. When Chase and Richard trade stories about Perkus during their night in jail together, Chase realizes that they are really talking about "that city Perkus had always chided me for failing to know," defined by Perkus's personal New York pantheon: Frank O'Hara, Joe Brainard, Jane Jacobs, Lenny Bruce, Andy Warhol, Jim Carroll, Jean-Michel Basquiat, Philippe Petit, and so forth (429–30). Chase adds Perkus's name to the list mentally, registering that with Perkus gone, he will never exactly know the precise city that Perkus knew and loved.

Of course *Chronic City*'s New York is not only a post-Giuliani New York; it is also a post-9/11 New York. The attacks on the World Trade Center are never directly invoked in the novel, but Lethem's frequent references to the "gray fog" that covers lower Manhattan invoke the attacks symbolically. The symbolism is rather clear, but "hints of a catastrophe that cannot be directly discussed are all that are permitted."[11] At a dinner party early in the novel, Chase sees on his hosts' wall a piece of art, "a crisp architectural-style rendering of a dark pit that plunged between two Manhattan office towers," which another guest identifies as a plan for Laird Noteless's project "*Expunged Building*" (*CC* 30). As another guest arrives, Chase sees "shreds of the gray fog still clinging to his creased pinstripe three-piece," invoking news photographs of ash-covered

New Yorkers fleeing the World Trade Center site (35). "I know I'm meant to feel we're all in something together, especially after the gray fog stretched out to cover the lower reaches of the island," Chase muses, invoking the sense of national togetherness in fall 2001—and the speed with which it dissolved (65). Later, Laird Noteless wins "the commission for the Memorial to Daylight [that] popular sentiment had demanded in reply to the gray fog downtown" (96). The city's color-coded tiger-watch system, meant to keep New Yorkers aware of the destructive tiger's whereabouts and potential for harm (226), clearly satirizes the Department of Homeland Security's post-9/11 threat-level system.

Samuel Cohen makes an intriguing case for reading *The Fortress of Solitude* as a post-9/11 novel (and imparts on it an even greater literary significance as such), a result of the open-endedness of its structure. Given that *The Fortress of Solitude* was published well after the victorious end of the Cold War and early in the manifold uncertainties of the war on terror, Cohen writes, "American stories that acknowledge the terror of the future and resist imposing closure on the past are becoming increasingly important."[12] Lethem has suggested that *Chronic City* "sort of centers in-between the two disasters, 9/11 and then the economic collapse, that defined the beginning and the end of this decade. And it's about being lost somewhere in between those two" (*Conv* 170). Even as characters do not reference either disaster directly, Lethem undergirds all of *Chronic City* with the uncertainty that Cohen describes. Countless witnesses to the towers' collapse claimed that what they saw looked like a movie. With that in mind, it may sound far-fetched at first to suggest that the virtuality of Yet Another World points to a slippage between what is understandably real and what is not. But then again, Lethem's symbolic invocations of national tragedies (and their unexplainability) definitely emphasize the difficulty that all of us have making sense of the world we inhabit.

Chronic City is about making sense of multiple worlds, and as such, it "is simultaneously a comedy and a tragedy and an elegy and a madly encoded map, printed on paper that you suspect has a third side."[13] In Perkus's moment of most personal tragedy, the loss of his apartment, he realizes that his acquaintance best equipped to make sense of the world is Biller, who is equally adept at navigating the real and the virtual worlds. He becomes, for Perkus, "the essential man" (*CC* 343). Chase, though, gets all of his illusions destroyed by Claire Carter, and he deduces near the novel's end that any attempt to separate reality from its opposite is doomed. "Our sphere of the real (call it Manhattan) was riddled with simulations, yet was the world at hand," he proclaims, but far more ruefully than Biller would (448–49). "The world was ersatz and actual, forged and faked, by ourselves and unseen others. Daring to attempt to absolutely sort fake from real was a folly," he continues (449), drawing a conclusion that also serves as one more plea from Lethem to tear down the wall separating science fiction from literary realism.

Where earlier Lethem novels downplay the reliability of conspiracy theories, *Chronic City* lets conspiratorial thought have free rein, and indeed some plot points in this novel are perhaps best understood as the results of conspiracies, broadly defined. For his own part, Lethem has called conspiracy theories a "betrayal of the complex and ambiguous and, most importantly, the uncontrolled nature of our experiences" (*Conv* 14). Lethem's view resembles that of Frank Minna in *Motherless Brooklyn*, who dismisses any thought of conspiracy with the phrase "Wheels within wheels," which Lionel recalls was "used exclusively to sneer at our notions of coincidence" (*MB* 74). Even as he thinks, "Conspiracies are a version of Tourette's syndrome," he dismisses the idea of conspiracy, asserting that "all conspiracies are ultimately solipsistic" (*MB* 178). *Chronic City*, however, is driven by conspiracies. In one of his first meetings with Chase, for instance, Perkus insists, "*The New Yorker*'s font was controlling," so much so that Perkus says he must retype *New Yorker* articles in full before he can read them for himself (*CC* 13). Chase later claims, "I'd never been drawn to conspiracy theories, not being smart (or high-functioning autistic) enough to nourish the mental maps they demanded," but he does feel that the most supremely desirable chaldron should somehow belong to everyone, not just to the wealthy mayor (*CC* 284). When he asks Perkus point-blank whether he sees himself as a conspiracy theorist, Perkus responds as disapprovingly as if "I'd said rock critic. The only conspiracy was a conspiracy of distraction" (*CC* 390), which fairly accurately recalls the conspiratorial uses to which the Canadian separatists in Wallace's *Infinite Jest* put the fatal entertainment.

Two more subtle references invoke notable contemporary conspiracy narratives even more overtly: following another early interaction with Perkus, Chase describes, "Where Perkus took me, in his ranting, in his enthusiasms, in his abrupt, improbable asides, was the world inside the world" (*CC* 27). The phrasing "world inside the world" is a direct lift from *Libra* (1988), Don DeLillo's historical refashioning of the JFK assassination and his most conspiratorial novel yet. The sentence "There is a world inside the world" appears four separate times in *Libra*, each time implying deep knowledge about reality that not every character can access. Much later, near novel's end, when Chase questions Claire Carter as to the full story of Yet Another World, Claire mysteriously advises him to "follow the money." Chase responds by "trac[ing] the origin of the surplus flooding my checking account," which he thought all along had been TV residuals. "The signatory was the treasurer of the Manhattan Reification Society, that shadowy philanthropic trust appointed to enact the city's little

Gnuppet shows," he learns (458). "Follow the money" is a fairly transparent borrowing of Deep Throat's advice to Bob Woodward and Carl Bernstein in the film (though not the 1974 print) version of the Watergate exposé *All the President's Men* (1976). Both borrowings suggest that Chase's experiences are nearly unexplainable without reference to larger political and monetary realities.

Lethem's skepticism about conspiracy momentarily aside, Chase does reveal near the novel's end that he has been part of a deception. The series of letters from Janice to Chase, published in widely read newspapers to great interest, were ghostwritten by Oona, and Chase has known this all along. Chase tells Richard Abneg the full story while they are in jail together the night of Perkus's death: he and Janice had grown up together and been teenage sweethearts, true enough, and she was an astronaut. He suspects, though, that Janice died in space quite a while back and that the elaborate, soap-operaesque story lines of her letters back home, which have come to include a tumor that required a foot amputation, were pure fiction. "It took a lot of melodrama to keep the War Free edition from seeming a tad thin," Chase figures (*CC* 459). He admits that some "callow producers" contacted him "long ago" about the ruse and has concluded that they, like Oona, must also be supported by the Manhattan Reification Society. In fact Lethem has already set up the whole story in chapter 4, where Chase recalls "a strange meeting with a couple of producers" who tempted him with "the role of a lifetime" and "proposed that it was my residual career, and my existence as a Manhattan gadabout, that made me so very perfect for the role in question" (64–65). Chase says that he asked to see a script, just to get rid of them, but never heard from them again. Within the New York of the novel, then, the entire saga was concocted as a distraction from more substantive realities. As readers holding all the clues in our hands early in the text but not encouraged to put them together until its final pages, we too have been distracted from the deception itself by Chase's digressions. Just like the chaldron, what once seemed mystical and romantic gets revealed to be a tool, used by the wealthy to maintain their privilege.

None of this yet explains the tiger entirely. When Chase asks Claire Carter point-blank, "Is the tiger . . . being used to destroy . . . the city's enemies?" she replies flippantly, "The tiger is a distraction" (*CC* 447). Chase is sufficiently chastened that he does not ask the obvious follow-up question: a distraction from *what*? When Richard attempts to explain to Perkus that the city is not trying to stop the mechanical tiger because many of the buildings it destroyed "were pretty much dead wood in the first place," Perkus shoots back, "That's how urban renewal works. . . . You find an excuse to bulldoze stuff so that the developers can come in" (164). Perkus sees the tiger, then, as a municipally approved tool of gentrification. Later, Richard will reveal that Perkus has been subletting Richard's own rent-controlled apartment for years and that "it wasn't going to last forever" (304). Chase is shocked at Richard's "eager[ness] to view the tiger as an envoy of real estate destiny" (304). Taken together, these details suggest that the tiger is a distraction from just how mercenary the city has become, given its interest in wiping "dead wood" right off the map. After hearing that Biller has become rich through Yet Another World, but before finding out that chaldrons exist only virtually, Perkus opts for New York over its cyberspace equivalent. He still finds New York "a thing of beauty, however compromised at its seams, however overrun with crass moola, however many zones were hocked to Disney or Trump" (341). He loves New York despite the presence of forces such as those represented by the tiger, but he does not turn a blind eye to them either.

None of the novel's discussion of the tiger, often proceeding in terms so ambiguous that a reader might reasonably dismiss the whole thing as a city's collective delusion, prepares us for Chase coming face-to-face with a monstrous animal in person near the end of the book. Enraged by grief after hearing of Perkus's death, Richard punches a policeman, which briefly lands him and Chase in jail. After Richard has called in some nebulous favor to get them freed, the two come upon a "giant escaped tiger . . . tall, a second-story tiger, though not as enormous as its legend" (*CC* 433). Chase sounds surprised to report that it was "languorous, hypnotic, serene" (433). Not content to have seen the apocryphal figure in the background of the entire novel, he now speculates that there must be more mystery unrevealed: "possibly there were two tigers, the famous and chaotic one that lit the tabloid frenzy, and this more dignified one, who showed itself to us alone" (434). And there is more.

Just as a dead man's hand shows up at the poker table near the end of *Motherless Brooklyn,* the final pages of *Chronic City* leave a vague threat visible in the background. The tiger has become old news. New Yorkers are now "more enamored lately with the coyotes that have been terrorizing joggers at the Central Park Reservoir" (*CC* 464). In addition Chase has developed a Yet Another World avatar who, with Biller's help, plans to "storm Claire Carter's redoubt and seize her cache of chaldrons" (465). They hope to create a virtual museum of chaldrons that will be equally accessible to all of the simulation's users, well after Richard had been "the first to bring Bolshevik rage into this pursuit—to propose seizing the chaldrons of the rich" (287). Still suspecting that *Obstinate Dust* held some key to explaining the "existential puzzle" ("What information was hidden in those pages? . . . I felt sure something fancy was going on"), Chase starts working his way through the tome "in Perkus's memory" (376, 465). The novel ends on notes of continued grief following Perkus's death, especially since Chase has failed at all of his attempts to determine fully what kind of world he inhabits.

Rivka Galchen's final judgment on *Chronic City* is a useful one because it reveals how, for its myriad idiosyncrasies and just plain weirdnesses, this novel ultimately affirms positive forces and critiques negative ones without ever denying how difficult this task can be. Truth, generosity, and human connection sound great (and they are); Lethem illuminates how hard it can be to affirm these ideas in daily lived reality. *Chronic City,* Galchen writes, "is a good (moral veneer of the word intended) fiction; part of the magic trick of its goodness, however, is that it contains exacting satires of the kinds of fictions we find in our reality which aren't good: War Free Editions of newspapers, the distracting-from-more-pressing-urban-problems melodrama of a beautiful fiancée astronaut lost in orbit, the theater of fear made of an enormous tiger conveniently destroying buildings that developers likely would be happy to see go anyhow—tidy fictions of news more than half written by money or crowd-think or raw power."[14] She argues that *Chronic City*'s admonition to its readers to value the real over the virtual (or the more prosaic and common misleading falsehood) works as a powerful corrective to contemporary ideologies and practices that seek to distract people from seeing the reality before their own eyes.

Read in this way, *Chronic City* becomes an inheritor of a wide variety of Western intellectual traditions, with implications both personal and political. Yes, as James Peacock writes, Lethem's fiction consistently "address[es] issues that are fundamental and eminently recognisable to any reader: loss and the concomitant yearning for a renewed sense of fellowship and community."[15] Even more so, given *Chronic City*'s insistence on viewing the world as it really is no matter how painful the revelation may be, the novel becomes a twenty-first-century equivalent to Plato's allegory of the cave. In its skepticism toward media representations of the world that encourage us to ignore visible tragedies, particularly in details such as the war-free newspaper, it is reminiscent of the Marxist critiques of popular culture launched by Frankfurt School cultural critics such as Max Horkheimer and Theodor Adorno. In its desire for language that speaks plain truths plainly, as opposed to the novel's deceptive and flowery fake letters from Janice, it recalls George Orwell's "Politics and the English Language." More than any other fiction he has yet produced, *Chronic City* lets Lethem function as a social critic. This trajectory has continued through his most recent books, in which he works both as a perceptive critic with wide-ranging tastes, and—for the first time—as a writer of the realist historical novel.

CHAPTER 5

Recent Lethem

The Critic and the Realist

In *Chronic City,* Jonathan Lethem created a picture of contemporary New York City that constantly bears a sense that all is not right with the world. It is his most paranoid novel by a long shot. Since he had already made waves as a cultural critic with the 2007 publication of "The Ecstasy of Influence" in *Harper's,* it should come as no surprise that Lethem's next major work published after *Chronic City* explores another narrative of urban paranoia from a smart, highbrow-meets-lowbrow-meets-no-brow critical perspective.

In *Chronic City,* Lethem engages in some sharp satire in small moments, not generally underlining these moments of social critique as such. The optional "war-free" edition of the *New York Times* would be one; another would be Perkus Tooth's illicit residence in the Friendreth Canine Apartments, suggesting as it does that contemporary America sometimes appears to take better care of homeless animals than it does homeless people. Lethem admits that for any writer looking for images that can represent injustice in contemporary America, "it's almost impossible not to find easy targets. . . . And yet," he continues, "we all go on reading that newspaper, we all go on moving through our days. . . . Everything is as exaggerated and hysterically out of whack, and yet somehow the machine tumbles forward, day to day, and we wake up and take our positions inside it. Well, that's an interesting subject and an elusive one. The social satire is not elusive at all. All you have to do is take it to the ultimate degree and then you've got John Carpenter's *They Live* or [Mike Judge's film imagining a devolved future America] *Idiocracy.* And then you've said it as stridently as you possibly can" (*Conv* 181). As strident as *They Live* might be, it became the focus of Lethem's first book-length piece of criticism.

They Live (2010), a short monograph that performs some clever close reading of John Carpenter's 1988 anticonsumerist sci-fi satire of the same name, makes a strong case that even the most ephemeral-seeming pieces of pop entertainment can bear ideological import. *They Live* is the initial publication in Soft Skull Press's Deep Focus series, which seeks to produce thoughtful writing about genre movies and cult films not acclaimed enough to be thought of as essential masterpieces but not so schlocky that they have entered the canon of "so bad it's good" classics. To illustrate further the sensibility of the series, Christopher Sorrentino, Lethem's collaborator on the pseudonymous *Believeniks!*, has published a volume on the Charles Bronson vigilante drama *Death Wish*, for example. In the new century there has been an explosion in the market for and the popularity of smart, accessible, semiacademic, semiautobiographical pop criticism. This mode of writing is founded on the belief that even the most ephemeral-seeming pop artifacts can, in the right hands, support thoughtful, even revelatory analysis. Lethem's *They Live* is his first major work of this sort.

Before explaining the film's plot or characters in any detail, Lethem admits, "No offense, but *They Live* is probably the stupidest film ever to take ideology as its explicit subject. It's also probably the most fun" (*They Live* 7). An unabashedly nutty and paranoid sci-fi action comedy, *They Live* works from the core conceit that a pair of mysterious sunglasses allows our main character, a Los Angeles drifter played by the pro wrestler Roddy Piper, to see the world as it really is. Slick advertising reveals itself as uncomplicated, (literally) black-and-white messages to "obey" and "consume," while authority figures and well-heeled white-collar professionals are actually ghoulish aliens under all that makeup and power. Carpenter's screenplay was based on the 1963 short story "Eight O'Clock in the Morning," by the sci-fi writer Ray Nelson, a close friend of Philip K. Dick; Lethem's interest in the film surely owes much to its genre roots and near connection to Dick. Yet Lethem also unearths the cultural connections that make *They Live,* in his view, a more genuinely and complexly satirical film than his aforementioned characterization of its stridency would imply. He historicizes the film adroitly, explaining how it interacts with cultural contexts ranging from Ted Turner's 1980s plans to colorize classic American films to the "die yuppie scum" anger of New York's 1988 Tompkins Square Park riot, which occurred just three months before *They Live*'s theatrical premiere.

Unsurprisingly, the book also serves as a sharp study of influence. Lethem reveals the echoes of Hitchcock, Godard, and John Ford in *They Live,* sometimes making use of juxtaposed film stills in order to illustrate his comparisons fully. The book also shows Lethem at his most academic: Lethem bounces his reading of *They Live* against the work of, to name just a few, Slavoj Žižek, Roland Barthes, and Leslie Fiedler. The latter seems particularly significant for readers of Lethem's fiction, as Lethem briefly reads *They Live*'s central cross-racial friendship through the lens of Fiedler's influential reading of *The Adventures of Huckleberry Finn* as containing veiled homoeroticism, which is an equally provocative touchstone for understanding Dylan and Mingus in *The Fortress of Solitude.*

Lethem's next book-length piece of pop criticism, an entry in Continuum Press's long-running and respected 33 1/3 series, would come from a far more personal place. Each 33 1/3 volume analyzes in detail one great rock, pop, soul, or country album; Lethem's book on *Fear of Music* (2012) discusses the 1979 album of the same name by the highly influential new wave band Talking Heads. A slightly defensive, mock-serious author's note opens the book; it is akin to Twain's tongue-in-cheek "Notice" at the beginning of his *Adventures of Huckleberry Finn,* which famously threatens bodily harm against those who seek to overinterpret the novel ahead. Lethem's "Warning" reads, "Contents under pressure of interpretation. User may suffer unwanted effect vis-à-vis a cherished cultural token" (*Fear of Music* vii). Lethem's sort-of flippant warning admits that revisiting the artistic loves of one's childhood is a dangerous proposition—as Dylan Ebdus surely knew—and indeed *Fear of Music* is alone in Lethem's body of work in how it occasionally attempts to draw a boundary around its author's experience that does not admit visitors.

In the essay "The Beards" in *The Disappointment Artist,* Lethem recalls how fully he associated his own identity with the art that he loved as a young man and that would influence him as a mature writer: "Attempting to burrow and disappear into the admiration of certain works of art, I tried to make such deep and pure identification that my integrity as a human self would become optional, a vestige of my relationship to the art" (*TDA* 141). In this essay his love of *Fear of Music* becomes the prime example of his desire to become fully one with his cultural loves. "At the peak" of his identification with Talking Heads, Lethem recalls, "my identification was so complete that I might have wished to wear the album *Fear of Music* in place of my head so as to be more clearly seen by those around me" (*TDA* 139). But exactly what is being more clearly seen? This idea that in order to know someone fully one must understand his or her cultural reference points gets taken to its extremes in *Chronic City,* as Perkus Tooth finds most of his human interaction in the first half of the novel in meandering conversations consisting of book and movie recommendations. As Lethem has just critiqued this notion, though, by also emphasizing how much experience Perkus has blocked out of his life and how solipsistic his worldview has become, it is surprising to see Lethem lapse into a few Perkus-like moments in *Fear of Music.*

Lethem opens the book by describing a radio spot for the album *Fear of Music,* built around digital manipulation of the speaking voice of lead singer David Byrne, that aired in the New York area in 1979. After describing the advertisement, Lethem cautions, "Don't go fishing for this experience in the infosea; it isn't there to be found. Those of us who received the original transmission have had to make do with our cargo cult recollections for three decades now, and counting" (*FoM* ix). The last sentence there is unusual in Lethem's body of work because it is the rare moment in which Lethem claims a cultural artifact as more his than the reader's. Lethem's yen for sharing his influences and cultural obsessions with the reader is, at heart, connectional: he seeks not to lord his taste or his status as a connoisseur over the reader but instead to celebrate aesthetic experiences that, often, are equally available to readers. Naturally, this state of affairs is made possible by the existence of what Lethem calls "the infosea" above: the massive archive of cultural production to which we have access via the Internet. In fact, with a few skillful searches, the radio ad that Lethem describes *can* be found on the Web, at least in part; but then again he asserts there that what cannot be rediscovered is the *experience* of hearing that ad, alone in one's bedroom in 1979. It is one of the rare points in *Fear of Music* that does not entirely succeed, in my reading, because there Lethem privileges his own aesthetic experience at the expense of that of a potential reader. Similarly, elsewhere in the book, in seeking to answer the title question of a later chapter called "Is *Fear of Music* a New York album?," Lethem implies that New Yorkers are best suited to understand the record, in part because its tracks got more radio play in New York than elsewhere and because "the rest of the country" might not recognize the New York rock clubs name-checked in "Life during Wartime" (*FoM* 62)—as if it were impossible to have heard of a music venue in another city. In essence, Lethem suggests that because he was the right age, in the right city, at the right time, he understands this album better than the reader ever could. He will later claim that after the better-selling Talking Heads album *Speaking in Tongues* was released four years later, "The band 'belonged' to others now, the way *Fear of Music* belonged to me" (*FoM* 136). Lethem comes perilously close to the tired hipster plaint of *I liked them before everyone else did, before they were cool* or the like. Moves such as these, admittedly small moments in an insightful book, still come dangerously close to the aggressively personal criticism of a Dylan Ebdus or a Perkus Tooth, for which Lethem has shown at least a touch of disdain in his fiction.

Lethem admits the limitations of how he approached the art he loved in his youth; in that essay in *The Disappointment Artist,* he concludes, "I asked too much of them. . . . At the depths I'd plumb them, so many perfectly sufficient works of art would become thin, anemic" (*TDA* 142). Lethem plumbs the depths of *Fear of Music* in ways that illuminate this unusual record instead of killing it through dissection as though it is a biological specimen on a lab table. Indeed it is a delightful read for the Talking Heads fan and a thoroughly useful one for a reader wanting to understand Lethem's aesthetic and relationship to his influences more clearly. His articulation of a personal definition of the term "science fiction" is as clear a statement on the subject as Lethem has given us, and the book is at its most convincing in its suggestion that the paranoid mode exemplified by *Fear of Music* (and, I would add, much of *Chronic City*) is a useful, proud, and necessary artistic tradition. As he puts it, "paranoid art is the ultimate opposite, the urgent opposite, of complacent art" (*FoM* 109).

Though distrust of authority and rejection of complacency run throughout Lethem's most recent novel, *Dissident Gardens* (2013), I would not argue that it works in the paranoid mode. Instead its characters' active questioning of the status quo makes it Lethem's most overtly political work yet. Nearly every character in the novel can be termed a subversive (or more politely, perhaps, a progressive) in one way or another. Rose Zimmer is a proud communist; her daughter Miriam becomes an activist in her own way in the 1960s, supporting civil rights efforts and eventually going on an ill-advised trip to Nicaragua in naive support of the Sandinistas, a trip that results in her death and that of her husband, Tommy. Rose has an affair with Douglas Lookins, an African American New York policeman, after which both Rose and Miriam separately take the policeman's legitimate son Cicero under their wing. In the chapters of the novel closest to our present, Tommy and Miriam's orphaned son Sergius, raised at a Quaker school, will seek out Cicero, now an academic, as Sergius searches for information about the mother he barely remembers.

Structurally, *Dissident Gardens* may well be Lethem's most sophisticated novel yet. Though every bit as chronologically fractured as *Motherless Brooklyn* and *The Fortress of Solitude, Dissident Gardens* is presented as made up of separate, entirely independent, and cohesive stories with their own titles. When woven together, the chapters form a multigenerational saga. This is a new organizational scheme in Lethem's fiction, though one that will be familiar to readers of novels, such as Jennifer Egan's *A Visit from the Goon Squad,* that require readers to draw connections actively in order to integrate multiple plot lines.

Certain recurring features in Lethem's body of work continue to show up in *Dissident Gardens.* Lethem incorporates autobiographical elements again while never creating characters who are fully analogues of people in his life. In *The Disappointment Artist*, Lethem recalls that his maternal grandfather "fled his wife and New York when my mother was three, to repatriate in East Germany" (*TDA* 87). Rose's husband Albert does the same. Lethem's grandmother "was another secular Jew and defiant leftist" (*TDA* 87), which is a description as usefully concise as one could mount of Rose Zimmer.

The autobiographical energy in *The Fortress of Solitude* tends toward depiction of Lethem and his father the painter, and while Lethem has acknowledged that the book "does describe some aspects of my own father/son relationship," it should not be taken as straight autobiography by any means (*Conv* 90). Lethem models Miriam Zimmer, to a point once again, on his mother, Judith, as comparisons of *Dissident Gardens* with Lethem's remembrances in *The Disappointment Artist* reveal. Lethem's mother "pierced ears, with a pin and ice cube, at a jewelry shop" in Greenwich Village and "palled around with folksingers" (*TDA* 87); so does Miriam (*DG* 168). Lethem recalls his mother moving supermarket produce that had been picked by "exploited migrant workers" into the freezer section to be destroyed (*TDA* 91); Miriam does the same (*DG* 130). Lethem's mother was part of the "Capitol Steps Thirteen," who were "wrongly arrested during a Washington, D.C., protest for occupying what the ACLU would later prove, in a lawsuit on their behalf, to be public space" (*TDA* 97); Lethem attributes this past to Miriam Zimmer, who particularly relishes the detail of slapping against the wall the baloney from the sandwiches they were given in jail, just as Lethem writes of his mother (*DG* 113). As with *The Fortress of Solitude,* of course, readers should be careful not to take the autobiographical reading too far.

Lethem also takes inspiration somewhat liberally from existing cultural artifacts, performing creative appropriation just as he describes in "The Ecstasy of Influence." When Lethem has Miriam appear as a contestant on the quiz show *The Who, What, or Where Game,* he borrows material from an actual episode of the program; as I write this, the episode is still searchable and viewable on YouTube. Miriam's fictional opponents do not share names with the real contestants, nor does Lethem's game have the same outcome as the game in question. However, the chapter's sequence of trivia categories, entire questions, and even some wrong answers are pulled straight from the recorded reality of this show. One can also read the chapter as a nod to David Foster Wallace's "Little Expressionless Animals," a brilliant story of a female quiz show contestant who encounters questions that seem pointed directly at her and force her to reflect on her past, though Wallace's character is a far more successful contestant than is Lethem's. The chapter could also be seen as influenced by Wallace's "My Appearance," the story of a B-list actress's appearance on David Letterman's late-night show, some of whose dialogue was lifted from an actual Letterman interview, much to the consternation of Wallace's editors.

Elsewhere in *Dissident Gardens,* though, creative appropriation still gets viewed skeptically if it appears that such appropriation bears an air of condescension. When Miriam meets Tommy Gogan, he is singing with his two brothers as an Irish folk act. Tommy considers himself the artiste of the group, though; once thought of as "the sincere one," he became "the protest one" after his politics came to the fore in his songwriting (*DG* 160, 164). After Miriam persuades him to help make a pot of coffee for the homeless men living near them (*DG* 172–74), Tommy begins interviewing them for work on a wildly ill-advised concept album about Bowery bums called *Bowery of the Forgotten: A Blues Cycle* (*DG* 177). One "P.K. Tooth," reportedly just seventeen years of age (and hence clearly *Chronic City*'s Perkus Tooth; the chronology more or less checks out), calls it "a nauseous amalgam of keening country-blues ingratiation and arch poetry, larded through with platitudinous pity toward its subject matter" (*DG* 186). The record's poor reception essentially kills Tommy's career.

Like *As She Climbed across the Table* and *The Fortress of Solitude, Dissident Gardens* includes an academic, Cicero Lookins, in its cast of characters. He teaches at Maine's fictional Baginstock College and is well aware of his status as the college's "miraculous triple token, gay, black, and overweight" (*DG* 48). Sergius Gogan sits in on Cicero's seminar on "Disgust and Proximity" (*DG* 195), and Cicero is awkwardly ineffectual as he tries to get his students to open up about their relationships with their mothers, clearly hiding something himself. Cicero's insular academicism recalls Dylan Ebdus's description of academic culture at Berkeley, emphasizing the "unreadable tomes" of the university's "roster of black-clad theorists" *(TFoS* 313). An even better comparison may be Philip Engstrand in *As She Climbed across the Table,* who gives up traditional anthropology in favor of the study of "academic environments," where he finds opportunities to apply "information theory to the course catalogs, the reading lists, the food-service menus" (7–8).

Other features of *Dissident Gardens* signal concerns that are new in Lethem's body of work or new takes on elements that have appeared before. References to Judaism in Lethem's work had long been either cryptically subtle or dismissive. In the former case, consider Lionel Essrog's last name in *Motherless Brooklyn,* the esrog, Peacock reminds us, "being a citrus fruit used at the harvest festival of Sukkoth."[1] While Dylan Ebdus's girlfriend Abby in *The Fortress of Solitude* comments, "I thought you always said that the fact that you happened to be Jewish was, like, the *least* defining thing about you" *(TFoS* 460), Rose and Miriam are both defined in terms of their Judaism, or more accurately their active rejection of religious Jewish practice, which Dylan simply neglects more passively. This is made most visible and literal in the detail of Rose rather violently "chipping the mezuzah from her doorway with a screwdriver, gouging wood and scarring paint" (*DG* 92). Even so, such actions testify less to Rose's rejection of faith and more to her desire to be a good communist, "the party-made New Woman" (*DG* 92).

In its emphasis on how leftist thought and action have changed in America over several decades, *Dissident Gardens* has close literary cousins in grand historical novels by the likes of E. L. Doctorow (particularly *Ragtime* and *The Book of Daniel*) and Philip Roth (definitely *American Pastoral*). That said, Lethem takes pains to emphasize the limits of activist fervor. Miriam's application to go to the Deep South with CORE during Freedom Summer is rejected, as the organization she seeks to join (rightly) suspects that she will come across as too overbearing and unwilling to do the listening that is a vital part of racial reconciliation work (*DG* 122–25). Tommy Gogan's well-intentioned but naive record fails. Rose's cousin Lenny mounts an equally naive pitch to Bill Shea trying to convince him that the team that will become the New York Mets ought to be the Sunnyside Pros, Pros being short for Proletarians (*DG* 81). In addition Sergius Gogan, as a child, has taken the lessons of Quaker nonviolence so earnestly to heart that while he plays one game at a video arcade for hours, he never lets the plane he controls get hit but also never fires at the game's enemies (*DG* 306). Taken together, such failures do not at all suggest that these characters are upholding untenable political positions. Instead they highlight the considerable difficulties, not impossibilities, that people of progressive worldviews encounter in their attempts to turn their beliefs from abstractions to realities, from the mid-twentieth century to the present.

Like *Chronic City, Dissident Gardens* concerns reality far more than it does abstraction. The most unusual aspect of this novel, compared to Lethem's earlier fiction, is its complete lack of a fantastic element: no magical ring, no mechanical tiger, no virtual realities. The element that comes closest to the fantastic here, Rose's conversations with *All in the Family*'s Archie Bunker and the unlikely romance she finds with him after the death of Douglas Lookins, may well be entirely imagined anyway. In her later years, we know, Rose suffers from memory loss and does not recognize all of her visitors, so her talks with Archie may be the beginnings of senility as opposed to any literal going through the televisual looking glass. This shift to realism may be unexpected, given Lethem's career-long interest in breaking down the barriers between sci-fi and mainstream literary fiction, but for close readers of *Chronic City,* it should not come as a surprise. *Chronic City* expresses quite the active preference for the real over the virtual, as Lethem reveals at novel's end the deception behind much of the perceived slippage between reality and its opposite. *Dissident Gardens* emphasizes the ways that the most earnest attempts to effect change can go wrong if approached with unsophisticated romanticism.

Lethem's most recent book, the 2015 collection *Lucky Alan and Other Stories,* provides further display of Lethem's general shift from speculative or nonrealistic fiction to more strictly realist fare. The collection's nine stories were all previously published from 2006 to 2014. They appear out of chronological order in *Lucky Alan,* but rearranging them chronologically confirms this gradual movement away from Lethem's genre roots and into the literary mainstream (indeed the majority of this volume's stories debuted in the *New Yorker*). The collection's earliest story, "Their Back Pages," which originally appeared in *Conjunctions* in 2006, imagines a variety of comic book character types (e.g., a monster, a stereotypical villain, a generic nuclear family, and a rabbit) stranded, *Gilligan's Island*–style, on a deserted island following a plane crash. Here Lethem performs some expert appropriation and reuse of existing material, riffing not on specific characters but on archetypal figures and medium-specific tropes of comic-book storytelling. Murkly Finger, the villain, can read the collected stories of his equally semifictional neighbors in omnibus editions of their respective comics, while at story's end, two characters are left to survive only "on thought balloons, which they swallowed as soon as they arose, without opening their mouths" (*Lucky Alan* 90). The visual grammar of the comic book collides with the narrative logic of the deserted island tale.

The volume's latest stories, "The Porn Critic" and "Pending Vegan," which appeared in the *New Yorker* in April 2012 and April 2014, respectively, include no strictly fantastical elements, though they use kooky and eccentric narrators to depict idiosyncratic worlds. Kromer, the main character of "The Porn Critic," reviews adult films for the newsletter of a store called Sex Machines. He lives in a small space crammed full of media, but, unlike Perkus Tooth's bookshelves or Dylan Ebdus's wall of CDs, Kromer's "VHS cartons stacking up" are not a welcome entry point into Kromer's mind, as they can cause physical sickness, he discovers (*Lucky Alan* 100). A female acquaintance feels genuinely attacked by his archive, comparing visiting Kromer to "sitting inside a copy of *Guernica*" before rushing to the bathroom (100). Kromer soon understands that to many, his "special literacy . . . was positively toxic, able to compel vomit from gorgeous women" (103). The more sympathetic title character of "Pending Vegan" has renamed himself in half-hearted prophecy of the more conscientious person he aims to become eventually. While on a family vacation, he experiences Sea World as surrealistic and vaguely threatening, in part because he chooses to experience it without his prescription antidepressant. The story's critique of the maritime-themed amusement park on both ethical and aesthetic grounds recalls Perkus's frustration in *Chronic City* with the Disneyfication of New York City, but this story's animals are all definitely animals—no mechanical tigers or the like are to be found here.

In between, chronologically speaking, are other stories involving characters who make quixotic and bizarre decisions, but few involve entry into a speculative or nonrealistic world. Mystery tends to overwhelm the possibility of explanation. Out of sheer fandom (a kind of ecstasy of influence), the protagonists of "The King of Sentences" follow a beloved but reclusive writer to the small town where he lives; he agrees to meet them in a hotel, where he asks them to disrobe. They do, and he destroys their clothing—end of story. As "Procedure in Plain Air" opens, some mysterious workmen cut a hole in a sidewalk and imprison a man in it, under some newly laid planks of plywood. A bystander gets pressed into service protecting and feeding the trapped man, without any indication of who the prisoner or workmen are or why any of this is happening. In "Empty Room" a city family moves to a sprawling house in the country, where their patriarch decides one room must be left permanently empty and scheduled for individual, temporary use. Eventually his son rebels by sleeping with his college girlfriend in the empty room, later wondering to his sister in the story's final sentence, "Haven't you ever wondered . . . how much stuff we could fit in here, if we tried?" (*Lucky Alan* 121). Given Lethem's set of interests, the question can be read as a provocation: how many books, records, movies, and influences could one bring into the mind's empty room?

Two decades into a prolific and multifaceted career, Jonathan Lethem has produced novels, stories, and nonfiction that seek to do nothing short of altering their readers' perspectives on the visible world. He accomplishes this by questioning the extent to which an artificial, imagined barrier between speculative and realist fiction reflects the actual experiences of readers, not many of whom live on only one side of that divide. All the while Lethem has demonstrated that strong writing in either mode can speak to real-world questions of race, class, and cultural politics. Science fiction can support clear-eyed, pragmatic discussions of both big-picture and small-scale political concerns, Lethem reminds us, just as realist fiction need not remain too strictly tied only to the tangible and verisimilitudinous.

Lethem attacks that barrier largely by frequently incorporating into his work elements borrowed from many narrative modes that have impacted his reading life since childhood. At the top of this list would be detective fiction and sci-fi, but also in the mix are the western, the bildungsroman, the campus novel, the rock 'n' roll novel, and the multigenerational historical saga. Additionally Lethem embraces a literary aesthetic that does not just seek to hide its borrowings but reveals them openly and celebrates them instead. Uninterested in viewing these influences as a weighty past that one must rise above in order to attain artistic maturity, Lethem enters into conversation with his influences instead. In so doing, he necessarily depicts characters who take on a variety of attitudes in relation to the art and entertainment that they love and under whose influence they willingly live, from unabashed fandom to thoughtful critique. In the experiences of some characters, such as Lionel Essrog, identification with an artistic mode leads to the formation of an identity that helps one make sense of bewildering personal circumstances. In Perkus Tooth's case, ecstatic consumption of art and culture leads to increasingly self-centered withdrawal from the world, as opposed to more passionate engagement with the world. Dylan Ebdus lies somewhere between Lionel and Perkus on this spectrum, as enthusiastic fandom leads him to self-selecting communities whose efficacy he then questions. In all cases Lethem unearths and emphasizes the varied and unexpected ways that audiences and consumers put art to use in their lives.

Lethem has put to use the artworks that have helped shape his life's work by embracing their power and never running from their influence. His desires to be a creative appropriator, a bridge across gaps separating communities of readers, and yes, a tasteful curator have led to volumes of fiction and nonfiction that wear their influences openly and proudly. The arc of Lethem's career suggests a trajectory that moves from the fantastic to the realist, particularly when taking *Dissident Gardens* into account; but at the same time, other recent novels and nonfiction suggest a sustained interest in oddity and paranoia that is not going anywhere. Lethem is nothing if not unpredictable, so I will not hazard a guess where he will take readers next. Past evidence suggests, however, that it could be a library or a movie theater, a single block of a city street or another planet entirely, the future or the past.

NOTES

Chapter 1—Understanding Jonathan Lethem

1. Galchen, "In Between the Dream and the Doorknob," 168.
2. Hughes, "Into the Thickets," 252.
3. Ibid., 253.
4. Bloom, *The Anxiety of Influence,* 30.
5. Ibid., 5.
6. Ibid., xxii, xxiii.
7. Ibid., 94.
8. Ibid., xxiii.
9. Ibid., xxv.
10. Ibid., 12.
11. Ibid., 13.
12. Ibid., 96.
13. Ibid., 10.
14. Barth, "The Literature of Exhaustion," 29.
15. Ibid., 31.
16. Ibid.
17. Ibid., 33.
18. Barth, "The Literature of Replenishment," 71.
19. Ibid., 70.
20. Chabon, "Fan Fictions," 56–57.
21. Ibid., 57.
22. Dinnen, "In the Mix," 219.
23. Kandel, "Is Something New Happening," 6.
24. Barth, "The Literature of Exhaustion," 30.
25. Farber, "White Elephant Art," 234.
26. Ibid., 240.
27. Ibid., 241.

Chapter 2—*Motherless Brooklyn:* Self-Aware Influence and Stylized Genre

1. Peacock, *Jonathan Lethem,* 95–96.
2. Chandler, "The Simple Art of Murder," 977.
3. Ibid., 982–83.
4. Ibid., 988.
5. Ibid., 988–89.
6. Chandler, "Twelve Notes on the Mystery Story," 1004.

7. Fleissner, "Symptomatology and the Novel," 390.
8. Chandler, "The Simple Art of Murder," 991.
9. Peacock, *Jonathan Lethem,* 98.
10. Chandler, *The Lady in the Lake,* 3.
11. Chandler, *The Long Goodbye,* 422, 424.
12. Hammett, *The Maltese Falcon,* 580–81.
13. Ibid., 582.
14. Peacock, *Jonathan Lethem,* 107.
15. Ibid., 104.
16. Chandler, "Twelve Notes on the Mystery Story," 1006.
17. Peacock, *Jonathan Lethem,* 111.
18. Ibid., 112.

Chapter 3—*The Fortress of Solitude:* Experience and Interpretation

1. Peacock, *Jonathan Lethem,* 121.
2. Leonard, "Welcome to New Dork," 32.
3. Hughes, "Into the Thickets," 252.
4. Godbey, "Gentrification, Authenticity, and White Middle-Class Identity," 136.
5. Hughes, "Into the Thickets," 240.
6. Ibid., 241, 251.
7. Ibid., 241.
8. Ibid., 255.
9. Peacock, "Jonathan Lethem's Genre Evolutions," 440.
10. Hughes, "Into the Thickets," 254.
11. Coughlan, "Jonathan Lethem's *The Fortress of Solitude* and *Omega*," 196.
12. Ibid., 199.
13. Singer, "Embodiments of the Real," 276.
14. Peacock, *Jonathan Lethem,* 124.
15. Ibid., 123.
16. Hebdige, *Subculture,* 115.
17. Ibid., 116–17.
18. Hughes, "Into the Thickets," 252.
19. Ibid., 252.
20. Peacock, *Jonathan Lethem,* 129.
21. Bourdieu, *Distinction,* 60.
22. Peacock, *Jonathan Lethem,* 131.
23. Hughes, "Into the Thickets," 258.
24. Ibid., 258.
25. Cohen, *After the End of History,* 4.
26. Godbey, "Gentrification, Authenticity, and White Middle-Class Identity," 147.
27. Davis, "High, Low, and Lethem," 65.
28. Cohen, *After the End of History,* 180.
29. Ibid., 183–84.

Chapter 4—*Chronic City:* Ecstatic Appreciation and Its Discontents

1. Peacock, *Jonathan Lethem,* 116.
2. Petty, "Narrative Transformations," 105.

3. This background information on Lethem's innovative plan regarding the film rights to *You Don't Love Me Yet* was taken from a page on an older version of Lethem's personal Web site, then located at http://www.jonathanlethem.com/freelove.html; it is accessible through the Internet Archive's "Wayback Machine" at http://www.archive.org. Last accessed September 1, 2014.

4. Galchen, "In Between the Dream and the Doorknob," 170.

5. Ibid., 171.

6. This short piece is available on Lethem's Web site, at http://www.jonathanlethem.com/perkustooth.htm. Last accessed September 1, 2014.

7. McHale, *Postmodernist Fiction,* 10.

8. Reynolds, *Retromania,* 129.

9. Ibid., 129.

10. Ibid., 141.

11. Peacock, *Jonathan Lethem,* 152.

12. Cohen, *After the End of History,* 186.

13. Galchen, "In Between the Dream and the Doorknob," 163.

14. Ibid., 178.

15. Peacock, *Jonathan Lethem,* 169.

Chapter 5—Recent Lethem: The Critic and the Realist

1. Peacock, *Jonathan Lethem,* 114.

BIBLIOGRAPHY

Fiction by Jonathan Lethem

Gun, with Occasional Music. New York: Harcourt Brace, 1994.

Amnesia Moon. New York: Harcourt Brace, 1995.

The Wall of the Sky, the Wall of the Eye. New York: Harcourt Brace, 1996.

As She Climbed across the Table. New York: Doubleday, 1997.

Girl in Landscape. New York: Doubleday, 1998.

Motherless Brooklyn. New York: Doubleday, 1999.

This Shape We're In. Brooklyn, N.Y.: McSweeneys, 2000.

Kafka Americana [with Carter Scholz]. New York: W. W. Norton, 2001.

The Fortress of Solitude. New York: Doubleday, 2003.

Men and Cartoons. New York: Doubleday, 2004.

Believeniks!: 2005: The Year We Wrote a Book about the Mets [with Christopher Sorrentino, under the pen names "Ivan Felt and Harris Conklin"]. New York: Doubleday, 2006.

How We Got Insipid. Burton, Mich.: Subterranean Press, 2006.

You Don't Love Me Yet. New York: Doubleday, 2007.

Omega the Unknown [story by Jonathan Lethem and Karl Rusnak, artwork by Farel Dalrymple and Paul Hornschemeier]. New York: Marvel, 2008.

Chronic City. New York: Doubleday, 2009.

Dissident Gardens. New York: Doubleday, 2013.

Lucky Alan: And Other Stories. New York: Doubleday, 2015.

Nonfiction by Jonathan Lethem, including Edited Work

The Vintage Book of Amnesia: An Anthology of Writing on the Subject of Memory Loss. Ed. Jonathan Lethem. New York: Vintage, 2000.

Da Capo Best Music Writing 2002: The Year's Finest Writing on Rock, Pop, Jazz, Country & More. Ed. Jonathan Lethem. Cambridge, Mass.: Da Capo, 2002.

The Disappointment Artist. New York: Doubleday, 2005.

Philip K. Dick: Four Novels of the 1960s. Ed. Jonathan Lethem. New York: Library of America, 2007.

Philip K. Dick: Five Novels of the 1960s and 1970s. Ed. Jonathan Lethem. New York: Library of America, 2008.

Philip K. Dick: VALIS and Other Late Novels. Ed. Jonathan Lethem. New York: Library of America, 2009.

They Live. New York: Soft Skull Press, 2010.

The Ecstasy of Influence: Nonfictions, Etc. New York: Doubleday, 2011.

The Exegesis of Philip K. Dick. Ed. Pamela Jackson and Jonathan Lethem. Boston: Houghton Mifflin Harcourt, 2011.

Fear of Music. New York: Continuum, 2012.

As of September 1, 2014, more information about Lethem's Promiscuous Materials project is available at http://www.jonathanlethem.com/promiscuous.html.

Secondary Works

BOOKS AND ESSAYS

Bloom, Harold. *The Anxiety of Influence*. 2nd ed. New York: Oxford University Press, 1997.

Bourdieu, Pierre. *Distinction: A Social Critique of the Judgment of Taste*. Trans. Richard Nice. Cambridge, Mass.: Harvard University Press, 1984.

Chabon, Michael. "Fan Fictions: On Sherlock Holmes." In his *Maps and Legends*, 35–57. San Francisco: McSweeneys, 2008.

Chandler, Raymond. *The Lady in the Lake*. In *Raymond Chandler: Later Novels and Other Writings*, ed. Frank McShane, 1–200. New York: Library of America, 1995.

———. *The Long Goodbye*. In *Raymond Chandler: Later Novels and Other Writings*, ed. Frank McShane, 417–734. New York: Library of America, 1995.

———. "The Simple Art of Murder." In *Raymond Chandler: Later Novels and Other Writings*, ed. Frank McShane, 977–92. New York: Library of America, 1995.

———. "Twelve Notes on the Mystery Story." In *Raymond Chandler: Later Novels and Other Writings*, ed. Frank McShane, 1004–11. New York: Library of America, 1995.

Clarke, Jaime, ed. *Conversations with Jonathan Lethem*. Jackson: University Press of Mississippi, 2011.

Cohen, Samuel S. *After the End of History: American Fiction in the 1990s*. Iowa City: University of Iowa Press, 2009.

Farber, Manny. "White Elephant Art vs. Termite Art." In *American Movie Critics: An Anthology from the Silents until Now*, ed. Philip Lopate, 233–41. New York: Library of America, 2008.

Hammett, Dashiell. *The Maltese Falcon*. In *Dashiell Hammett: Complete Novels*, ed. Steven Marcus, 387–586. New York: Library of America, 1999.

Hebdige, Dick. *Subculture: The Meaning of Style*. 1979. London: Routledge, 1988.

Hughes, Evan. "Into the Thickets of Urban Crisis." In his *Literary Brooklyn: The Writers of Brooklyn and the Story of American City Life*, 239–58. New York: Henry Holt, 2011.

McHale, Brian. *Postmodernist Fiction*. London: Routledge, 1987.

Peacock, James. *Jonathan Lethem*. Manchester: Manchester University Press, 2012.

Reynolds, Simon. *Retromania: Pop Culture's Addiction to Its Own Past*. New York: Faber and Faber, 2011.

CRITICAL ARTICLES

Barth, John. "The Literature of Exhaustion." *Atlantic*, August 1967, 29–34.

———. "The Literature of Replenishment." *Atlantic*, January 1980, 65–71.

Coughlan, David. "Jonathan Lethem's *The Fortress of Solitude* and *Omega: The Unknown*, a Comic Book Series." *College Literature* 38.3 (2011): 194–218.

Davis, Ray. "High, Low, and Lethem." *Genre* 42.3–4 (2009): 61–78.

Dinnen, Zara. "In the Mix: The Potential Convergence of Literature and New Media in Jonathan Lethem's 'The Ecstasy of Influence.'" *Journal of Narrative Theory* 42.2 (2012): 212–30.

Fleissner, Jennifer L. "Symptomatology and the Novel." *Novel: A Forum on Fiction* 42.3 (2009): 387–92.

Galchen, Rivka. "In Between the Dream and the Doorknob: On Jonathan Lethem's Fictions." *Ecotone* 5.1 (2009): 162–80.

Garrison, John. "Echoes of Influence: Music, Social Power, and the Law in Speculative Fiction." *Journal of the Fantastic in the Arts* 17.4 (2007): 321–33.

Godbey, Matt. "Gentrification, Authenticity, and White Middle-Class Identity in Jonathan Lethem's *The Fortress of Solitude*." *Arizona Quarterly* 64.1 (2008): 131–51.

Kandel, Michael. "Is Something New Happening in Science Fiction?" *Science-Fiction Studies* 25.1 (1998): 1–6.

Leonard, John. "Welcome to New Dork." *New York Review of Books,* April 7, 2005, 31–34.

Peacock, James. "Jonathan Lethem's Genre Evolutions." *Journal of American Studies* 43.3 (2009): 425–40.

Petty, William. "Narrative Transformations: Jonathan Lethem's *Men and Cartoons,* Comic Books and Geek Culture." *Popular Culture Review* 17.2 (2006): 101–13.

Rossi, Umberto. "From Dick to Lethem: The Dickian Legacy, Postmodernism, and Avant-Pop in Jonathan Lethem's *Amnesia Moon*." *Science Fiction Studies* 29.1 (2002): 15–33.

Singer, Marc. "Embodiments of the Real: The Counterlinguistic Turn in the Comic-Book Novel." *Critique* 49.3 (2008): 273–89.

INDEX

ABOUT THE AUTHOR

MATTHEW LUTER is on the English faculty at the Webb School of Knoxville in Tennessee. He has published articles on Don DeLillo, Ellen Douglas, Bret Easton Ellis, and Amiri Baraka, among others.